THIS BOOK BELONGS TO

For my daughter, Gwendolyn, and my husband, Perry

Thanks to the following people for their expertise: To the many kids who were expert readers and enthusiastic craft testers, especially Gwen, Tommy, Elizabeth, Evan, Jack, and Juliet. Anne Wright for copy editing and testing crafts with her daughter Alice, Kathryn Kuchenbrod for copy editing and proofing, and Julie C. Grant for her charming watercolor illustrations.

Special thanks to B.J. Berti, my editor at St. Martin's Press, who cut paper stars when needed, and for making this book possible.

Picture Credits:

Pages 17, 24, 51, 52, 54, 57, 58, 65, 69, 74, 83, 84, 85, 99, 100, 102, 106, 125, 126, 127, 131, 135, 136: Julie C. Grant; page 24: Hal Rasmusson, magazine illustration, undated; page 44: Miriam Story Hurford, magazine illustration,1926; page 80: Maginel Wright Barney, courtesy of Nicholas Gillham; page 96: unknown, magazine cover, 1924; page 117: seed packet art courtesy of D. Landreth Seed Company; pages 108,112: Maginel Wright Barney, courtesy of Nicholas Gillham; page 127: Ernest Crichlow, from *Two is a Team*,1945.

Crafting Fun

101 Things to Make
and Do with Kids

Rae Grant

St. Martin's Griffin
New York

Also by Rae Grant:

Cooking Fun:121 Simple Recipes to Make with Kids

www.stmartins.com

Written and designed by Rae Grant

Compilation copyright © 2008 by Rae Grant

Every effort has been made to obtain permission from publishers and copyright holders. Credit, when known, is listed on page 2.

Library of Congress Cataloging-in-Publication Data Available Upon Request

ISBN-13: 978-0-312-37780-9

ISBN-10: 0-312-37780-0

First Edition: October 2008

10 9 8 7 6 5 4 3 2 1

A Note to Families

Crafting Fun: 101 Things to Make and Do with Kids is a collection of classic childhood projects that kids and families can use all year long. It's a ticket back to a less busy time, and a reminder of how much fun it can be to make and do simple things.

In our hurried times, it's a full-time job for families to accomplish all the necessary tasks in a given week, let alone pull out paper and glue to make a craft project with the kids. Sometimes, we just need a few good ideas to get us started. This book is here to help.

Organized by season, *Crafting Fun* will introduce kids of all ages to classic childhood crafts that parents and grandparents may well recall. Many of these charming projects can be made using simple household materials. Kids can celebrate the seasons by making a pumpkin-seed necklace (see page 32) crayoned waxed leaves for fall (see page 12), cut paper snowflakes during the winter holidays (see page 58) or make a hand-bound summer scrapbook (see page 134).

Fun things start to happen when kids sit down at the table and make a craft. Like a family dinner, crafting brings kids and parents together and allows for a quality time that the TV or computer just can't provide.

So get your kids and their friends together and form a craft club. Serve a snack, do a project, tell stories, and have fun crafting the old-fashioned way!

Happy crafting!
Rae Grant

www.craftingfunforkids.com

Table of Contents

Spring

Summer

Useful Throwaways

Here's a list of the many useful items you can recycle to use for crafting.
Many of the projects in this book can be made with simple household items
like paper, string, aluminum foil, buttons, cookie cutters, and milk cartons.

PAPERS

Aluminum foil
Brown paper bags,
    various sizes and
    weights
Construction paper
Cardboard
Crepe paper
Decorative cardboard
Decorative paper
Envelopes, various sizes
Handmade paper
Newspaper
Old calendars
Old greeting cards
    and postcards
Origami paper
Paper catalogues
Paper plates
Paper doilies
Paper napkins
Poster board
Recycled paper
Stickers
Telephone book
Tissue paper
Tracing paper
Wallpaper
Plain white paper

CONTAINERS

Berry basket
Straw garden basket
Cardboard salt box
Cardboard gift box,
    various shapes and sizes
Cardboard tubes
Candy box
Candy or cookie tin
Cereal box
Coca tin
Coffee can with lid
Egg carton
Glass jar, baby food,
    jam and jelly jars,
    mason jars with lids
Oatmeal container
Old perfume bottles
Pie tins
Plastic spray bottles
Matchboxes
Milk carton, plastic
    and cardboard of
    varying sizes
Plastic cups
Shoe box
Metal soup cans,
    cleaned

FABRICS

Cheesecloth
Clean, worn dish towels
Felt and fabric scraps
Old scarves, mittens
    and gloves
Ribbon
Shoelaces
String from shopping bags
Twine
Worn cotton pillowcases
    and sheets
Worn pants and shirts
Worn shirt and pant
    pockets
Yarn

ODDS AND ENDS

Balloons
Bells
Binder clips
Bottle caps
Bottle corks
Buttons
Candles
Coat hanger
Cotton balls

Drinking straws
Erasers
Feathers, from craft stores
Ice cream sticks
Magnet
Nails
Paperclips
Paper cups
Pinecones
Pipe cleaners
Pom-poms
Postage stamps (used)
Push pins
Safety pins
Sea shells
Seed packets, empty
Sequins
Spools, plastic and wooden
String
Thread
Toothpicks
Rubber bands
Wooden chopsticks
Wooden clothespin
Wooden dowel
Wooden frame

Getting Started

Ask an adult if you can make a workspace in the kitchen, a private room, or an unused corner. Set it up to be your special crafting area. Keep your tools and materials well organized. Store materials on a shelf, in a drawer, or in a large plastic storage box. You can make your own smaller storage containers from everyday items like an empty shoebox, oatmeal container, or coffee can. Use them to hold pencils, crayons, rubber stamps, fabric scraps, bottle caps, buttons, or even a rock collection. When you're finished working, put your material away in the same place each time. It's always nice to come back to a clean and organized workspace.

Safety First

All of these projects require adult supervision, especially when using sharp tools, any electrical appliances, or matches. When you see the words ADULT HELP NEEDED in the directions, ask an adult for assistance. Safety is the top rule to follow when crafting.

Basic Equipment Needed

Clear tape	Ink pad	Scissors	Electric blender
Compass	Markers	Stapler and staples	Hammer
Colored pencils	Masking tape	String	Rolling pin
Construction paper	Measuring tape	Tracing paper	Rotary egg beater
Craft knife	Needle and thread	Watercolor paints	Sauce pan
Craft paint	Newspapers	Waxed paper	Sandpaper
Crayons	Paintbrushes	White glue	Screwdriver
Eraser	Pencil		Serrated knife
Glitter	Pencil sharpener	**Extra Material**	Smock or apron
Glue stick	Plain white paper	Bowls and cups	Spoons
Hole punch	Rubber stamps	Cookie cutter	Vegetable peeler
Household sponge	Ruler	Cookie sheet	Window screening

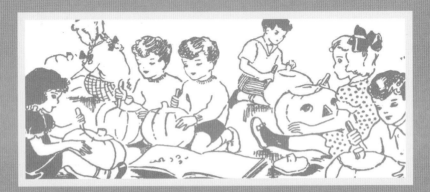

Autumn

Autumn Projects

September

Waxed Paper Leaves

Apple Print T-Shirts

Paper Bag Book Cover
(and more)

Apple Candle Holders

October

Scarecrow

Paper Jack-O'-Lantern

Simple Halloween Mask

Tin Can Lanterns (and a
Good Ghost Story)

Halloween Silhouette Cut-Outs

Spooky Cheesecloth Ghosts

Handkerchief Ghosts

Glitter Pumpkins

Pumpkin Seed Necklace

Roasting Pumpkin Seeds

November

Corn Husk Cornucopia

Pinecone Turkey

Thanksgiving Place Card

The First Thanksgiving

Toss-and-Catch Toy

Autumn Leaf Collecting

Skeleton Leaf Prints

U.S. State Tree Chart

Waxed Paper Leaves

*With this simple craft, you can preserve colorful autumn leaves and enjoy
them all year. Try melting colorful crayon shavings in between the waxed paper and leaves
for an extra splash of color. **Adult Help is needed when using a hot iron.***

Materials Needed

Autumn leaves of varying sizes and shapes

Newspapers

Scissors

Waxed paper cut in 8-inch squares
(2 pieces for each hanging)

Ironing board or covered tabletop

Crayons (red, orange, yellow, and green)

Pencil sharpener

Iron

Paper punch

Yarn or string

1. Collect autumn leaves. If they are damp, lay them flat on newspaper and allow to dry overnight.

2. Cover the ironing board with several layers of newspaper to protect the surface. Have an adult set the iron to a medium heat, no steam.

3. Use scissors to trim waxed paper in 8-inch squares. You'll need 2 per hanging. Make a pile of colorful crayon shavings on a paper plate.

4. Place a sheet of waxed paper on top of the newspapers. Arrange several leaves in a pattern on the waxed paper. Sprinkle a thin layer of crayon shavings across the leaves, then cover with a second sheet of waxed paper.

5. Cover waxed paper with another layer of newspaper and place iron on top. **With Adult Help,** hold iron in place for about 30 seconds until the crayon wax has melted and the waxed paper sheets stick together.

6. Let cool completely, then use a paper punch to make a hole in the top center of the square. Loop a string through the hole and tie in a knot. Hang in a sunny window.

Extra Ideas: Make several leaf pictures using leaves of different shapes and sizes. After you press the waxed paper, use scissors to trim along the shape of the leaf. String several waxed leaves together and drape across a window.

Apple Print T-Shirts

Celebrate fall by going apple picking and making a creative T-shirt. Experiment with different apple shapes and colors. Be sure to use crisp, fresh fruit for printing. You can also stamp on white or light-colored canvas bags, sneakers, white pillowcases, and paper.

Materials Needed

Plastic to cover the painting table
and a drop cloth for the floor

Newspapers

Cardboard

Smock

Apples

Paring knife

Shallow saucers for paints

White T-shirt

Fast-drying acrylic fabric paints

Coat hangers or clothespins

Sponges

Water for cleanup

1. Prepare your workspace by placing plastic over the work table and spreading newspapers or a drop cloth on the floor.

2. With Adult Help, use a paring knife to cut apple in half through the stem. Drain on a paper towel to soak up excess juice.

3. Place a flat piece of cardboard inside the shirt to prevent paint from bleeding through to the back of the T-shirt.

4. Pour various colors of paint into the saucers. Dip the apple in the paint and press firmly on the front of the fabric. Lift the apple and repeat until you have a design that you like. Redip the apple in the paint if necessary.

5. Hang the T-shirt on a hanger or clothesline to dry. For best results, T-shirt should dry for at least 1 hour or, if possible, overnight in a warm room.

Extra Ideas: Use natural objects such as autumn leaves, evergreen branches, sliced butternut squash, and even a whole fish to make colorful prints.

Paper Bag Book Cover (and more)

Make protective covers for all your schoolbooks using a brown grocery bag and a few paper-folding tricks. Once you learn this technique of folding, get creative and use an old travel map or sturdy decorative paper to cover all your favorite books. Your books will look great at the end of the year and you've recycled a brown bag at the same time.

Materials Needed

Sturdy paper bag or a roll of brown parcel paper

Pencil

Book

1. Starting at a top corner of the bag, cut along the crease to the base of the bag. Next, cut around 3 sides of the bottom flap until you have a large rectangular piece of paper (Fig. 1).

2. Set the book in the center of the paper and use a pencil to draw a line across the top and bottom of the book. Remove the book and crease the lines to make an even fold (Fig. 2). The fold should be as tall as your book. Crease well with your fingers or the edge of a ruler.

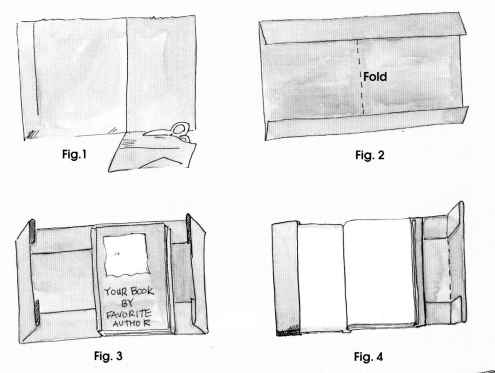

Fig.1

Fig. 2

Fig. 3

Fig. 4

3. Place the book in the center of the folded paper (Fig. 3). Take the left side of the paper and fold it over and around the front cover of the book to make a flap. Crease the edge. The flap should reach one-fourth of the way across the inside book cover. If it is too long, trim the flap to fit.

4. Insert the front cover into the slot created by the folded paper until you reach the crease (Fig. 4). Repeat for the other side.

5. Close the front cover of the book, pulling the paper tight across the front of the book (Fig. 5).

Fig. 5

Apple Candle Holder

Apple picking and autumn celebrations go together. Make the most of the extra apples by carving candle holders from fresh apples. Carve out stripes, zigzags, circles, or stars right into the apple peel. If you make some a day before a party, refrigerate to keep them from wilting. Be sure to ask an adult to supervise the candle lighting.

Materials Needed

Large apples (ones that will sit evenly on a table)

Vegetable peeler or paring knife

Candle (1 for each apple)

Aluminum foil

Lemon juice

1. With Adult Help, use the point of a vegetable peeler to make a hole at the top of the apple. Carve in about halfway through the middle of the apple core and make the hole a little wider than the candle. Remove the core piece and discard.

2. Decorate the apple by carefully carving designs in the skin with the vegetable peeler. You can decorate the surface by just peeling lightly, or carve deeper by using the point of your peeler. When you like your design, rub the carving with lemon juice to prevent the apple from turning brown.

3. Insert a candle into the hole. It should fit tightly; if the hole is too large, wrap a band of aluminum foil around the base of the candle. Arrange the candle holder on a festive plate or tray. **With Adult Help,** light the candles.

Scarecrow

Traditionally, scarecrows kept unwanted birds, particularly crows, out of vegetable gardens and away from cornfields. Today, people often use them as part of their autumn and Halloween decorations. A homemade scarecrow can be made from old clothes stuffed with newspapers or fresh hay. Make it a group project and put together a really scary or friendly scarecrow.

Materials Needed

Long-sleeved flannel shirt

Old pair of pants or jeans

Twine

Newspapers, straw, or hay

Old pair of socks or boots

Gloves or mittens

Safety pins, medium and large

Belt

Pillowcase for the head

Pencil and markers for the face

Straw hat

1. To assemble your scarecrow, tie the bottom of the pant legs and the ends of the shirt sleeves with twine. Button the shirt and zip up the pants. Stuff the pants and shirt with crumpled-up newspaper until the legs and arms are plump. Next, stuff the socks and gloves with more newspapers, and tie the openings with twine.

2. Fasten the socks (or boots) and gloves to the inside of the pants and shirt with safety pins. Tuck the shirt into the pants. Tighten and buckle the belt around the "waist."

3. Use a pencil to outline the facial features of the scarecrow on the pillowcase, then fill in with paint. Next, stuff the pillowcase with newspapers and fasten it to the body with safety pins. Fasten the head firmly to the scarecrow shirt.

4. Place your scarecrow outside on bales of hay, or prop it up against a wall inside the hallway in your house.

Paper Jack-O'-Lantern

Tape a scary jack-o'-lantern inside a lampshade or in a window for Halloween. It's easy to make, so you might have time to make several—one for each lampshade and window!

Materials Needed

Orange construction paper

Black tissue paper

Brown or green construction paper (optional)

Clear tape

Scissors

Glue

1. Tape a sheet of orange construction paper and black tissue paper together and cut out a pumpkin shape. Separate the orange and black pumpkins.

2. Cut out eyes, a nose, and a mouth from the orange pumpkin. Fold the pumpkin face in half and cut out the details.
Don't worry if it isn't perfect. The scarier the better. Glue the black paper to the back of the orange pumpkin. Cut a stem and leaves out of brown or green paper, and glue them onto the pumpkin.

3. Tape the jack-o'-lantern on the inside of a lamp shade. When you turn on the light a spooky shadow will glow through the lamp shade. You can also hang it in the window on Halloween night.

Simple Halloween Mask

Make a Halloween mask from easy-to-find items around the house. Paper plates, paper bags, and cardboard boxes can be crafted to become a really unique costume.

Materials Needed

Craft paint

Paintbrush

White paper plate

Scissors

Construction paper

Glue

Paper punch

2 lengths of string, yarn, or ribbon

1. Paint the back side of the paper plate with a paintbrush or your fingers. Let dry completely.

2. Cut out eyes, nose, and mouth for your animal, as appropriate. Using construction paper, cut out ears and whiskers, if needed. Glue onto the inside top edge of the paper plate so it sticks out over the top. Let dry.

3. Paper punch a hole near the edge on opposite sides of the plate. Thread a string through each hole and tie in a simple knot. Leave enough string on either side so you can tie the mask around your head. When you put on the mask, tie the string in a bow so it can come off easily.

Tin Can Lanterns
(and a Good Ghost Story)

Candle lanterns can make an evening Halloween party very special. If you have a party, have all the guests sit in a room filled with glowing lanterns, and then have someone tell a good ghost story.

Materials Needed

Tin cans (cleaned and dried)

Permanent marker

Water

Freezer

Crayon

Towel

Nails of various sizes

Hammer

Small tea candles

1. With Adult Help, check each tin can for sharp edges before starting. Soak the can in hot soapy water. Peel and scrub off the labels.

2. Fill each can with water and place in the freezer overnight or until frozen solid.

3. Remove from freezer. Draw a design on the frozen can with a crayon or marker. Keep the design simple, such as an outline of a pumpkin face, or make random dots all over the can.

4. Place the can on its side, on top of a thick towel. Position a nail on a point in your pattern, and hammer a nail hole through each marked point. Experiment using different-size nails to create interesting effects when the lantern is lighted.

5. Allow the ice to melt. Towel-dry the inside of the can and then place a small tea candle in the base of each one. Set the lantern on a plate. **Have an adult light the candles,** then turn off the lights and tell a really good ghost story.

Halloween Silhouette Cut-Outs

Decorate your doors and windows with spooky black bats and cats. For a sturdier shape, trace template onto a piece of cardboard and use it as a backing for the paper cut-out. Glue it to one side of black paper before decorating.

Materials Needed

Tracing paper

Black construction paper

White colored pencil

Scissors

Glue

Orange glitter

Clear tape

Wooden craft stick or ice cream stick

1. Trace a black cat or bat shape (see page 26) onto white tracing paper and cut out. Place cut-out on black construction paper and outline the shape in white colored pencil. Cut along the white lines to get your shape.

2. Spread a thin line of glue along the edge of the image and sprinkle glitter or sequins along the line of glue. Outline the eyes, nose, and mouth with glue and decorate as you like. Tape the back of cut-out onto the top of a wooden stick. Use as party favors or costume props.

Extra Ideas: Glue smaller-size spooky cats and bats to the back of a standard wooden clothespin and let dry. Clip to the top of a decorated brown lunch bag. Be sure to add treats to the bag before closing.

Spooky Cheesecloth Ghosts

*Get into the spirit of Halloween and hang these very spooky ghosts
in your house, on the porch, or outside on a tree branch.*

Materials Needed

Newspapers

Balloons (1 per ghost)

Drinking glass

Cheesecloth, cut in 14-inch double-layer squares

Shallow bowl

1 tablespoon water

2 tablespoons glue

Needle and thread

1. Prepare your work surface with a thick pile of newspapers. Blow up the balloons
and set them in the drinking glasses; this will let you to mold the damp cheesecloth
in a ghostly shape that you like.

2. Cut squares of double-layer cheesecloth. In a shallow bowl make a mixture
using 2 tablespoons of glue and 1 tablespoon water. Dip the cheesecloth squares in
the glue mixture and squeeze out the excess glue into the bowl. Drape the cheesecloth
on the balloon in a ghostly shape of a flying or standing ghost. Let it dry overnight on
the glass.

3. When dry, draw in a ghostly face, then remove the balloon by popping it. Set the
ghost on a table top as a centerpiece or sew a thin thread through the back and hang
from a doorway or window.

Handkerchief Ghosts

Handkerchief ghosts are a Halloween favorite and are very easy to make.
If you don't have a white handkerchief, use fabric from a clean white
T-shirt, or use white sheets of tissue paper.

Materials Needed

Balloons (1 per ghost)

White handkerchiefs (these are easy to find in most drugstores)

Charcoal pencil or black marker

Thin black or white ribbon, about 4 inches long

Thread

1. Blow up the balloon so it is about the size of an orange. To make a ghost head, cover the balloon with the handkerchief. Next wrap a ribbon around the base of the balloon to form the head shape. After you tie a knot in the back of the head, you should have enough ribbon for hanging the ghost.

2. Use the charcoal pencil or marker to create a scary face on the ghost. When you are ready to hang the ghost in the window, tie a thread around the ribbon in the back of the head and hang in a window.

Glitter Pumpkins

These glistening pumpkins are sure to be a Halloween party favorite for kids, and they last longer than jack-o'-lanterns. Make them large or small and line them up on a mantle, table, or doorstep. You can even try glittering gourds and dried corn as well. Pumpkins will keep for several weeks indoors and for months when kept outdoors in cool weather.

Materials Needed

Newspapers and paper plates

Small bowls

Powder glitter in various colors
(orange, red, gold, brown)

Glue

Paintbrush

Spoon

Small pumpkin

1. For each pumpkin project set out newspapers and a paper plate to catch glitter. Fill each bowl with a different color of glitter.

2. Pour glue into a small bowl and stir in enough water to make glue smooth but still thick. Use a paintbrush to coat the surface of a pumpkin with glue. Hold pumpkin over a paper plate or a sheet of newspaper to catch excess glitter. Sprinkle glitter over pumpkin, working with one color at a time, covering the surface completely. Let dry for about 1 hour, then shake off excess glitter.

Pumpkin Seed Necklace

After carving the jack-o'-lantern save the seeds to make a traditional seed necklace. Try using natural dyes (see page 87) to color the seeds and string a colorful necklace that resembles traditional Indian corn. This is a great project for a Halloween party.

Materials Needed

Pumpkin

Wooden beads (optional)

Large bowl

Colander

Shallow cookie sheet

Bowl

Fishing line, about 24 inches long

Needle (with a large eye)

1. With Adult Help, remove the top of a pumpkin for carving. Use your hands or a strong metal spoon to scoop out pumpkins seeds and pulp from a pumpkin. Set pumpkin aside for carving. Place the seeds in a colander and carefully wash them to remove the pulp. Drain well. Place the seeds on a towel and pat dry. Spread the seeds on a baking sheet and set in the sun for several hours to dry. Scrape off any excess pulp when dried and place seeds in a bowl.

2. Thread fishing line through the needle and tie the end in a knot. Leave about 2 inches of string for tying the necklace around your neck.

3. Take one seed at a time and pierce the center of the seed with the needle. Pull the seed down along the needle and push down to the base of the knot. Next add a wooden bead and then another seed. Continue in this pattern until you have a full length of seeds for a necklace. When you are finished, tie the end of the string in a firm knot, leaving a 2-inch tail for tying the necklace around your neck. If you need to lengthen the necklace, tie a colorful string of embroidery thread to both ends of the string.

Roasting Pumpkin Seeds

Pumpkins, and their seeds, were a celebrated food of Native Americans. Pumpkin seeds were treasured for both their dietary and medicinal properties. After carving a pumpkin, ask an adult to help roast cleaned pumpkin seeds in a toaster oven. Lay seeds on a sheet of foil and sprinkle with salt and a small amount of olive oil. Roast on a low setting for 15 minutes or until toasted to a golden color. Serve as a snack.

Corn Husk Cornucopia

The native people of America offered corn to the Pilgrims as a gift of friendship and taught them how to grow it. This gift helped them survive the long cold winters. The Thanksgiving cornucopia, also known as a Horn of Plenty, is a symbol of abundance. Make a Thanksgiving cornucopia in the tradition of giving and offer it to a friend.

Materials Needed

1 sheet of 11-by-17-inch brown card stock
or heavy brown paper

Masking tape

2 to 3 ears of dried multicolored corn with husk
(or packaged corn husks used to make tamales)

Twine

Scissors

Tissue paper (brown, gold, or red)

Nuts, dried fruit, popcorn, and maple sugar candies

1. Take an 11-by-17-inch sheet of brown card stock or paper and roll it into a cone shape. Tape the seam with masking tape.

2. Bend the pointed end of the cone slightly to curve it into the shape of a horn, and wrap the entire cone with more tape to create a stiff cone.

3. Remove dried husks from the ears of corn stalks.

4. Take 4 to 6 strips of dried corn husks and layer them along the cone lengthwise until you have covered the entire cone. Wrap the base and center of the cone with twine to secure the husks.

5. Add cone-shaped tissue wrapping paper into the cone and fill with nuts, dried fruit, popcorn, and maple sugar candies. Use as a centerpiece for the Thanksgiving table or wrap in tissue paper and ribbon to bring as a house gift on Thanksgiving Day.

Extra Ideas: To make a colorful band, use a glue stick to attach corn kernels to the twine. Let dry before filling cone with treats.

Pinecone Turkey

Make a whole family of turkeys for the Thanksgiving Day table using small and large pinecones. Collect pinecones on walks in the park, or buy them at a craft store. Give them as party favors for guests to take home or use them to make place cards for Thanksgiving Day guests.

Materials Needed

1 sheet each yellow, orange, and red construction paper or felt

Dry pinecones of varying sizes

Feathers (craft stores sell these by the bag)

Glue

Pom-poms (1 per turkey)

Popcorn kernels, uncooked

1. For each turkey, cut out a yellow or orange beak from paper or felt. To make the beak, fold yellow construction paper and cut out a small double triangle, about 1 ½ inches along the fold. Cut a rounded L shape from red paper for the turkey's wattle.

2. Using 6 to 8 feathers per turkey, lightly dip the ends of the each feather into the glue. Insert it into the back of the pinecone to form a colorful turkey tail. Let dry.

3. Glue the pom-pom to the tip of a pinecone to form a head. Allow glue to dry. Next, glue the beak and a red wattle to the pom-pom. Add popcorn kernels for eyes.

Thanksgiving Place Card

Both big and little hands work well for this family craft.

Dip your hand in craft paint and make a colorful print, or trace your hand on red, yellow, or orange construction paper. Trim the shape and write the name of the guest in your best handwriting. Use alone to make a place card, or tuck the base of the hand into the back of a pinecone to form a colorful turkey tail.

The First Thanksgiving

*O*ur national holiday began as a feast held in the autumn of 1621 by the Pilgrims and members of the Pokanoket Tribe of the Wampanoag Nation. The Pokanoket Tribe were the native people of what we now call New England. It was a feast to celebrate the colony's first successful harvest. This is a list of what may have been the foods from the First Thanksgiving.

Fish: cod, bass, herring, shad, bluefish, and eel

Seafood: clams, lobsters, mussels, and very small quantities of oysters

Birds: wild turkey, goose, duck, crane, swan, partridge, eagle

Other Meats: venison (deer), possibly some salt pork or chicken

Grains: wheat flour, Indian corn and corn meal, barley

Fruits: raspberries, strawberries, grapes, plums, cherries, blueberries, currants, gooseberries

Vegetables and legumes: small quantities of leeks, onions, peas, squash (including pumpkins), and beans

Nuts: walnuts, chestnuts, acorns, hickory nuts

Herbs and Seasonings: brooklime, flax, liverwort, strawberry leaves, sorrel, watercress, and yarrow

Other Items: maple syrup, honey, butter, cheese, and eggs.

The Pilgrims may have brought seeds from England to plant radishes, lettuce, carrots, onions, and cabbage.

The 53 Pilgrims at the First Thanksgiving Dinner

The Pilgrims worked long and hard to survive the first year in their new home, which they called Plymouth, often suffering from hunger and serious illness. A great sickness caused the death of many family members and crew members of the ship on which they sailed. Here is a record of the names of the children and grown-ups who were fortunate enough to come together for a plentiful harvest feast in the fall of 1621.

5 Girls: Mary Chilton, Constance Hopkins, Priscilla Mullins, Elizabeth Tilley, and Dorothy, a maidservant.

9 Boys: Francis and John Billington, John Cooke, John Crackston, Samuel Fuller (2d), Giles Hopkins, William Latham, Joseph Rogers, Henry Samson.

13 Young Children: Bartholomew, Mary & Remember Allerton, Love and Wrestling Brewster, Humility Cooper, Samuel Eaton, Damaris and Oceanus Hopkins, Desire Minter, Richard More, Resolved and Peregrine White.

4 Adult Women: Eleanor Billington, Mary Brewster, Elizabeth Hopkins, Susanna White Winslow.

22 Adult Men: John Alden, Isaac Allerton, John Billington, William Bradford, William Brewster, Peter Brown, Francis Cooke, Edward Doty, Francis Eaton, (first name unknown) Ely, Samuel Fuller, Richard Gardiner, John Goodman, Stephen Hopkins, John Howland, Edward Lester, George Soule, Myles Standish, William Trevor, Richard Warren, Edward Winslow, Gilbert Winslow.

Toss-and-Catch Toy

This toy is simple to make, but you need a quick hand and sharp eyes to make it work. Used by children of the Pokanoket tribe, it may have been a game of skill for hunting and fishing. It a great tradition to have on Thanksgiving Day or any time of year.

Materials Needed

Cotton string or twine, about 24 inches long

Wooden stick, about 12 inches long

Vine (raffia, cattail reeds, or pumpkin vine), about 12 inches long

1. Tie a string around the middle of a stick and secure it with a knot. Take the piece of vine and twist to form a circle or hoop about 3 inches in diameter. Tie the other end of the string to the hoop and secure it with a tight knot.

2. To play the game, hold the stick in your hand and gently swing the hoop out and around. Try to catch the hoop with the top of the stick. Practice catching the hoop with both your left and right hands. For a challenge, turn the bottom of the stick upward to catch the hoop.

Autumn Leaf Collecting

Whether you live in the city or the country, you can begin to learn about your native or local trees by taking a walk outside. Autumn leaves can be collected during walks in parks and woodland areas, along quiet streets, and in back yards.

Materials Needed

Brown paper bag, an old magazine or book

Notebook

Colored pencils

Newspapers

Binder clips

1. When selecting leaves for a collection, look for leaves that are in perfect condition. Avoid leaves that have been torn or damaged. As you collect favorite leaves, place them in a brown bag or flat between the pages of a magazine or book to preserve them.

2. When you get home, make a simple leaf press to dry and flatten leaves. Cut newspaper into 8 ½-by-11-inch sheets. Stack sheets in a neat pile and bind one side together with clips. Place each leaf in a single layer between a sheet of newspaper. Let them dry until flat for 1 to 2 weeks.

Extra Ideas: Bring along a notebook or a special journal to use during your walk. Draw the shapes and colors of the leaves. Observe the characteristics of the trees as well as the leaves. Ask a parent, teacher, or librarian to help pick out a tree identification book and bring it along on your walk.

Skeleton Leaf Prints

Preserve the skeleton of your leaf by pounding away the fleshy parts of the leaf and make a card print or a bookmark at the same time.

Materials Needed

Wooden board

Sheet of white paper, any size

Fresh leaves

Palm-size rock or old soft-bristle hairbrush

1. Place a wooden board on a clean table surface. Place the paper on the wooden board and then place the leaf on top. Hold the leaf firmly with one hand and use a rock or soft-bristle brush to gently pound the surface of the leaf. Pound lightly for several minutes until the colored part of the leave is worn away. Turn the leaf over and pound the other side for a few minutes. The pounded leaf skin will print or transfer its shape onto the paper, leaving a lacy skeleton of veins.

2. To preserve your leaf skeleton; mount and label it in a homemade scrapbook (see page 134), display in a picture frame, or press between waxed paper (see page 12). Include your new print in the journal, or use it to make a decorative name plate or cover for your journal.

U.S. State Tree Chart

Alabama, Longleaf pine

Alaska, Sitka spruce

Arizona, Palo verde

Arkansas, Southern yellow pine (shortleaf pine)

California, California redwood

Colorado, Colorado blue spruce

Connecticut, White oak

District of Columbia, Scarlet oak

Delaware, American holly

Florida, Sabal palm

Georgia, Live oak

Guam, Ifil or ifit

Hawaii, Kukui or candlenut

Idaho, Western white pine

Illinois, White oak

Indiana, Tulip tree

Iowa, Oak

Kansas, Cottonwood

Kentucky, Tulip poplar

Louisiana, Bald cypress

Maine, Eastern white pine

Maryland, White oak

Massachusetts, American elm

Michigan, Eastern white pine

Minnesota, Red pine

Mississippi, Magnolia

Missouri, Flowering dogwood

Montana, Ponderosa pine

Nebraska, Cottonwood

Nevada, Single leaf pinion pine

New Hampshire, White birch

New Jersey, Northern red oak

New Mexico, Pinion pine

New York, Sugar maple

North Carolina, Longleaf pine

North Dakota, American elm

Northern Marianas, Flame tree

Ohio, Buckeye

Oklahoma, Redbud

Oregon, Douglas fir

Pennsylvania, Eastern hemlock

Puerto Rico, Silk-cotton tree

Pennsylvania, Eastern hemlock

Rhode Island, Red maple

South Carolina, Sable palm

South Dakota, Black Hills spruce

Tennessee, Tulip poplar

Texas, Pecan

Utah, Blue spruce

Vermont, Sugar maple

Virginia, Flowering dogwood

Washington, Western hemlock

West Virginia, Sugar maple

Wisconsin, Sugar maple

Wyoming, Plains cottonwood

Winter

Winter Projects

December

Snow Globe
Bend-Up Christmas Tree
Holiday Doorbell
Cut-Paper Garland
Paper Chain
Orange Pomander
Apple Pomander
Spiral Ornament
Tinsel Stars
Rolled Beeswax Candles
Beeswax Cut-Outs
Paper Snowflakes
Popcorn-and-Cranberry Garland
Perfect Popcorn
Ornament Cards
Wassail Bowl
Evergreen Door Decoration
Sparkly 3-D Christmas Tree
Glitter Pinecones
Christmas Card Holder
Greeting Card Garland

January

Holiday Tree for Birds
Hanging Baskets
Pinecone Treats
Outdoor Ice Picture
New Year's Eve Piñata
New Year's Party Favors

February

Valentine Envelope Cards
Invisible Ink
Rubber Stamp Hearts
Quick-Thinking Valentines
Valentine Carrier

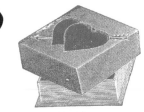

45

Snow Globe

Snow globes are a magical way to create a snowy winter storm in a jar. String a ribbon with several small jingle bells, and tie it around the outside of the lid. It will make a merry sound when you shake the jar.

Materials Needed

Small glass jar with lid
(baby food, and jam jars work well)

Florist clay (found at most craft supply stores)

Plastic or ceramic figurines of deer or evergreen tree

Distilled water or water that has been boiled and cooled

Glitter (found at most craft supply stores)

Glycerin or corn syrup

Glue

1. Wash and dry your jar completely, including the lid. Press florist clay around the inside of the lid to make the base. Gently push figurines into the clay to make an arrangement that you like.

2. Fill the jar with distilled water to within ½ inch of top. Add ¼ teaspoon of glycerin or corn syrup to help the glitter float slowly in the liquid. Sprinkle ½ teaspoon of glitter into the liquid. Screw the lid on tightly. Add a layer of glue around the outside edges of the lid to seal in the water. Allow glue to dry. Gently turn the jar over and back again to make it snow.

Bend-Up Christmas Tree

*Make a bend-up evergreen tree for a greeting card or tabletop decoration
that everyone will enjoy. You can draw as much detail as you like on the tree,
or keep it simple and draw the shape of the tree.*

Materials Needed

Pencils, some colored, for decorating

Tempera paints

White or colored construction paper
or cardboard, any size

Scissors or craft knife

1. Draw a large evergreen tree on the paper or cardboard with an attached base, as in picture. Decorate your tree using color pencils and paints. If you add more than one tree, leave a few inches of space around each tree.

2. **With Adult Help,** cut along the outline of the tree and the sides of the base. Leave the bottom base, where the tree bends, uncut. If you cut all the way across the bottom, the tree won't bend up. When you are done cutting, bend the tree shape up. Place on a table to enjoy or send it in an envelope as a present to someone special.

Holiday Doorbell

Make a musical doorknob wreath using colorful jingle bells,
which you can find at a craft shop. Hanging a long ribbon of bells
from a door knocker also makes a festive sound.

Materials Needed

Scissors

Ribbon, about 12 inches long

25 small jingle bells of various
sizes and colors

Embroidery thread, about 12 inches long

Count out about 25 small jingle bells. Thread bells onto the ribbon until you have enough to form the size of you want. Tie the ribbon in a knot and then a big bow. Slip it over a doorknob and enjoy the festive sounds it will make.

Extra Ideas: You can also make a musical ankle bracelet using jingle bells. You may want to use embroidery thread instead of ribbon for this project.

Cut-Paper Garland

Make a long paper chain to decorate your tree or doorway using only folded paper and scissors. Try using wrapping paper, colored tissue paper, or aluminum foil.

Materials Needed

8 ½-by-11-inch paper (green, red, multicolored, or shiny wrapping paper)

Scissors

1. Fold a sheet of paper in half lengthwise, then fold again lengthwise, back toward the first fold. You should have folds on both vertical edges. With your scissors, snip each side alternately. Be careful not to cut all the way across.

2. Carefully open the folded paper. Cut the sheet in half along the center fold line. Gently pull each strip apart slightly. You can attach the 2 strips together to form a longer garland if you like. Attach each end of the chain to a branch on the tree.

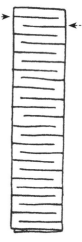

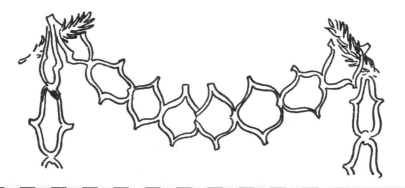

Paper Chain

Paper chains can be made extra fancy by gluing colored foil shapes and sequins to each link. Use paper in holiday colors or multicolored scraps of wrapping paper to make your chain bright and unique. For decorations, use sequins or cut aluminum foil in small wavy strips or star shapes. Glue the decorations to the outside of the links to make the chain sparkle.

Materials Needed

Scissors

Construction paper (green, red, or multicolored paper)

Pencil

Ruler

Glue stick or clear tape

1. Cut about 20 strips of paper, each measuring about 1 inch wide and 4 inches long. Use a pencil and a ruler to mark off your strips.

2. Roll a strip of paper into a circle, and glue or tape the edges together securely.

3. Put the next strip through the loop to form a new link, and glue or tape the second strip together as directed for the first. Continue until you have a chain long enough to hang across a doorway or the fireplace mantel. You might need to cut more strips.

Orange Pomander

A pomander is a ball of sweet-smelling fruit and spices that was originally worn around the neck to protect people from disease and bad smells. Now we make them to add spirit to the holidays and to fill our homes with sweet and spicy scents. Make orange pomanders in batches, and give them as holiday gifts.

Materials Needed

Masking tape

Orange or clementine

Small jar whole cloves

Small nail

Red ribbon or fabric trim, about 2 to 3 feet long

1. Wrap the masking tape around the orange as shown at right. Pour the cloves into a small bowl. Poke the thin end of each clove into the skin of the orange. If this is hard to do, poke a hole in the orange with a nail or a ballpoint pen then add the clove. Decorate the orange with as many of the remaining cloves as you want to make a nice pattern, keeping the cloves off the taped area.

2. Remove the tape and wrap the ribbon around the orange using the empty space from the masking tape as a guide. Tie the ends of the ribbon in a knot, leaving long ends, then form a loop with the ends. Tie a bow with a small piece of ribbon above the knot. Hang the orange from a strong branch on the Christmas tree or a hook in a window. A spicy orange scent will perfume the air. Enjoy!

Apple Pomander

To make an apple pomander, you will need an apple and a jar of cloves.
Prepare the apple with masking tape and poke cloves into the skin, just
as you did with the orange. When done, put 2 tablespoons each of
powdered cinnamon and ginger into a brown paper lunch bag. Add the
decorated apple to the bag. Close the bag and shake it until the apple is
coated with the spices. Remove the tape and tie a ribbon around as
described for the orange. Hang it in your window or on your Christmas tree.

Spiral Ornament

A spiral ornament can be made of any type of paper.
Experiment with different materials and see which one you prefer.
Send this as a gift in a colorful envelope. It mails flat but opens easily
to hang as an ornament.

Materials Needed

Silver paper

Red paper

Glue stick

Needle

Silver embroidery thread

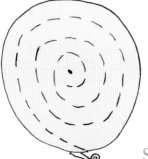
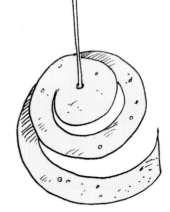

1. Layer two sheets of paper together and cut a 4-inch square. You will have 2 pieces of paper, 1 silver and 1 red.

2. Stack the squares evenly and glue back sides together. Beginning at a corner, cut the stack in a spiral shape until you reach the middle. Leave a knob or circle in the center.

3. Use a needle to sew a silver thread loop, either at the outside end or the center knob. You can also poke the end of a paper clip through the paper instead of using a needle and thread, and bend it to form a hanger.

Tinsel Stars

*Tinsel is charming and magical. Here's a very easy method
for twisting tinsel pipe cleaners into hanging stars. Add silver or gold colored
beads to the end of the pipe cleaner to make it glisten in the light.*

Materials Needed

6 standard tinsel pipe cleaners (silver, gold, or multicolored)

Beads (optional)

Scissors

1. Cut a standard pipe cleaner in half so you have 2 equal lengths. Cut a third pipe cleaner about ¼ inch longer than the other two pieces. This third piece will be the hook.

2. Twist the 2 equal pieces together at the centers, then wrap the third piece onto the twisted pieces, forming a star.

3. Bend the top end of the third piece into a hook and hang the ornament on tree. Repeat with the remaining pipe cleaner to make 2 more stars.

55

Rolled Beeswax Candles

Candles were once the only source of light in homes all over the world. In winter they light up the night with a soft glow and symbolize that winter will soon be over. Try making beeswax candles for any of the winter holidays. You can roll small ones for menorahs or roll one large candle for a traditional candlestick.

Materials Needed

2 sheets 8-by-16-inch honeycombed beeswax

Ruler

Wick (found at most craft stores)

Small paring knife or scissors

Ribbon or string for wrapping

1. Lay out 1 sheet of beeswax on a work surface that is safe to cut on. The wax should be room temperature. Use a ruler to measure 4-by-2-inch sections. Cut the wax into the sections you marked.

2. Cut a 5 ½-inch length of wick for each candle. Tie a small knot at one end of each wick.

3. Crease the edge of the wax sheet over the wick and press firmly so that it is well sealed. Next, gently roll the sheet tightly, making sure the ends are even. Continue to roll until you reach the end of the sheet.

4. Gently pinch the seam together to secure the shape of the candle. Continue with remaining wax and wicks until you have about 16 candles for each sheet. Tie a colorful ribbon or string around bundles of 4 or more candles.

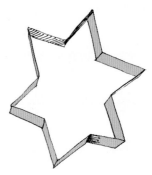

Beeswax Cut-Outs

Try making these ornaments using leftover beeswax sheets. Use various cookie cutters to make a collection of decorations. The beeswax sheets work best if they are at room temperature.

Materials Needed

Cookie cutters (birds, trees, stars, candles)

1 sheet 8-by-16-inch honeycombed beeswax

Nail or pencil

Thin ribbon or colorful embroidery thread

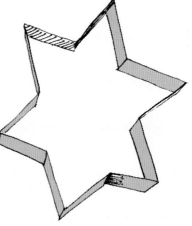

1. Select a cookie cutter and cut out shapes from your sheet of wax.

2. Using the nail, press a hole into the top of the cut-out. The hole should be large enough to slip the ribbon through. Tie the ribbon in a knot or a bow. Hang it in a window or on a tree, or wrap 2 or 3 as a gift.

Paper Snowflakes

Make a blizzard of paper snowflakes using these simple steps. Don't worry if your snowflakes aren't perfect—real snowflakes are always one-of-a-kind. Experiment with different square sizes, cuts, and snips, then decorate your bedroom, home, or classroom with snowflakes.

Materials Needed

Sturdy white paper

Scissor

Thread

Clear tape

1. To begin, fold a 8-inch square piece of paper in half diagonally to make a triangle (Fig. 1). Fold the triangle in half so the top point meets the bottom point (Fig. 2).

2. Next fold the triangle in thirds, or about to the dotted line as shown in Fig. 3.

3. Fold the outer flap (Fig. 3) back over the new fold (going from right to left). Your new shape will look like Fig. 4.

4. Turn the shape over and cut along the lower edge of the triangle just above the bottom points as shown in Fig. 5. Snip the edges and make a shape as shown in Fig. 6, or experiment with your own patterns. When done, unfold snowflake carefully. Tie a thread through the top. Tape thread to the top and hang in a window or use as a tree ornament.

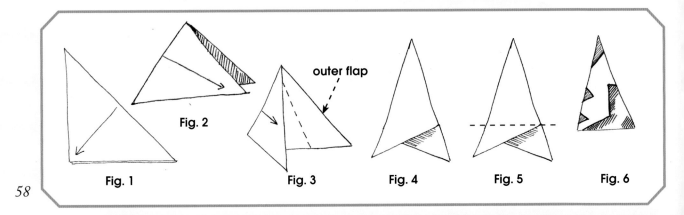

Fig. 2

outer flap

Fig. 1   Fig. 3   Fig. 4   Fig. 5   Fig. 6

Popcorn-and-Cranberry Garland

This holiday craft is a perfect reason to have a holiday decorating party. Invite friends and family over to help string popcorn garlands. Serve hot wassail (see page 63) and enjoy the holiday season together.

Materials Needed

1 large bowl of popcorn

1 bag of fresh cranberries

Needle

Thread

1. Measure 12-inch length of thread. **With Adult Help,** thread your needle. Tie a knot at the end.

2. Stick the point of the needle into middle of a kernel of popcorn and pull the thread through on the other side. The first few kernels may break, but keep trying until you get the hang of it. Push the first threaded kernel to the end of the thread. Continue adding until you have a string of popcorn and cranberries in a pattern that you like.

3. Once the garlands are done, tie the top of each string in a knot. Drape garlands across the boughs of your Christmas tree.

Perfect Popcorn

To make a perfect pot of stove-top popcorn, it's very important to shake the pan while the corn is popping. This helps prevent the cooked corn from sticking to the bottom of the pan. **Adult help required**.

Materials Needed

1 tablespoon vegetable oil

1 large pan with lid

¼ cup popcorn kernels

Pot holder

With Adult Help, place 1 tablespoon of oil in a large stainless steel pan with a lid. Add the popcorn kernels to cover the bottom of the pan and cover with lid. Cook over medium heat until the kernels begin to pop, about 3 to 4 minutes. Use a potholder to hold the handle and shake the pan over the heat. Shake until the popping sound stops. Immediately pour the popped corn into a large bowl. Allow the popcorn to cool before making the garlands. Makes 8 cups.

Buttered Popcorn

Making popcorn garlands is really fun if you also have a huge bowl of buttered popcorn to munch on while you work. After popping the corn, just add salt and melted butter to the batch you want to eat.

Ornament Cards

You don't have to buy greeting cards every year. Use favorite greeting cards from the year before to make new cards that can double as ornaments.

Materials Needed

Ornament-shaped cookie cutter

Old greeting cards

Glue stick

Scissors

Hole punch

Ribbon or string, about 4 inches long

1. Using any cookie cutter ornament as your template, trace a shape on a pretty portion of a greeting card. Trace around the outside of the template with a pencil, then cut out the ornament shape.

2. Punch a hole at the top of the ornament card, and thread a ribbon or string through the hole to form a loop for hanging. Wrap in colorful tissue paper or place in an envelope to give as a gift.

Extra Ideas: Make a decorative backing for the ornament by tracing the same shape using a different card pattern or a solid color of construction paper. Glue the shape to the back side of the other decorative shape so that both patterns are facing out.

Traditional wassail was a hot ale drink served
to carollers when they came calling on a cold winter
evening. If you have a carolling party at your house,
make your friends a bowl of hot wassail made
of apple cider. For a real treat, serve it with your
favorite holiday cookies.

Wassail Bowl

2 quarts apple cider

1 cup orange juice

½ cup lemon juice

1 tablespoon brown sugar

3 cinnamon sticks

1 teaspoon whole cloves

1 teaspoon ground ginger

Lemon and orange slices

1. Combine all the ingredients in a large saucepan. **With Adult Help,** turn on heat to medium-low until cider mixture is hot, about 10 minutes.

2. Ladle hot cider through a small strainer into mugs. If you like, after pouring in the hot cider place a cinnamon stick in each mug. Serves 8.

Evergreen Door Decoration

Hanging an evergreen branch on your door was once considered an invitation for woodland spirits to enter your home and bring prosperity to you and your family. Now we consider it a welcoming symbol during the Christmas holidays. Make a welcoming door hanging with evergreen branches or holly leaves and decorate it with small glitter pinecone (see page 66).

Materials Needed

2 to 5 medium-size evergreen branches

String

1 yard of 2- to 3-inch red ribbon

1. After trimming your tree, save a few of the best branches. Tie branches together by wrapping string around the cut ends several times until the branches are secured. Tie a large red bow around the string.

2. Add a loop of string in the back of the bow for hanging. Place on your door or in a window.

Extra Ideas: If you don't have a tree, check with your local tree sellers. They often have small branches for sale. You can also use holly and other evergreens.

Sparkly 3-D Christmas Tree

Materials Needed

2 sheets of 8 ½-by-11-inch green construction paper

Scissors or craft knife

Glue

Silver and gold glitter

1. Fold together two sheets of construction paper in half lengthwise. Draw an outline of one side of a Christmas tree. Be sure that the center of the tree runs along the fold line.

2. Cut out the tree shape through both pieces of paper, leaving the fold uncut. Unfold the trees. You should have 2 separate trees. Place small dots of glue on each tree, then sprinkle with glitter. Shake off excess glitter and let dry.

3. Along the fold of one of the trees, cut a slit halfway up from the base to the middle. On the second tree, cut a slit from the top to the middle. Insert the top slot into the bottom slot and open. You may have to adjust the slits.

4. To make a base for your tree, cut a piece of light cardboard in the shape of a circle or square. Use scissors or a craft knife to make crisscross slots in the center of the shape. Gently slip your assembled tree into the slots and adjust to make it stand.

Glitter Pinecones

Collect or buy pinecones and get out the glitter!
This is always a holiday favorite. Hang them on
a holiday tree, or place a small branch in a vase, and
decorate it with glitter pinecones.

Materials Needed

Pinecones

Newspapers

Glitter (various colors)

Empty jar or small bowls

Glue

Paintbrush

Spoon

Paper plate

Thread

1. Cover your work surface with newspapers. Place a tablespoon of each color of glitter in separate bowls.

2. Pour several tablespoons of glue in a clean bowl and add about a teaspoon of water to thin it out. Working with one pinecone at a time, use a paintbrush to paint glue over the entire pinecone.

3. Using a spoon, hold the pinecone over a paper plate and sprinkle with glitter until the pinecone is well coated. Shake off the excess glitter onto the paper plate. Let the pinecone dry. Pour any extra glitter back into a small jar.

4. Tie a colorful thread about 5 inches long around the middle of the pinecone and make a loop. Hang it on your Christmas tree or use it as decoration on a wrapped gift.

Extra Ideas: Make a glitter pinecone tree by adding sequins and small colorful beads to the tips of the pinecone. Set the tree on a small mirror and decorate it with soft, white fabric or cotton stuffing to resemble an outdoor ice skating pond.

Christmas Card Holder

Collect and keep all of your holiday greeting cards in this decorative box. You can make the box very festive or keep it simple. Either way, you'll have a nice place to save and display all of your holiday cards.

Materials Needed

Scissors

1 cardboard box large enough to hold your cards
(an empty cereal box or pasta box works well)

Clear tape

2 sheets of red construction paper

2 sheets green construction paper or felt

Cotton balls

Glue

Markers and colored pencils

1. Cut off the top flaps of the box. Tape the bottom and sides of the box closed.

2. Cut 2 stocking shapes out of red construction paper that are as tall as your box. Glue the shapes onto either side of the box, making sure that the top of the stocking is at the opening of the box. Glue cotton balls at the top for added decoration.

3. Cut 2 strips of green construction paper or felt the width of your box and glue them to the uncovered sides of the box. Decorate as you like. Fill the bottom of the box with newspaper or wrapping tissue to help the cards pop out at the top.

Greeting Card Garland

Make a colorful display of greeting cards as a garland of ribbon and cards.
Wrap around a banister, or drape across the fireplace mantel or doorway.

Punch holes in each card in varying positions, and thread ribbon through the holes, making a chain of ribbons. Add two or three cards to the same ribbon to make a full display of cards. String jingle bells or shiny beads between cards. You can add more cards throughout the holiday by attaching more ribbon to the end of the garland.

Extra Ideas: You can also display favorite cards on a long red ribbon. Cut lengths of wide ribbon. Attach cards to the ribbon using paper clips or painted clothespins.

Holiday Tree for Birds

Share your holiday bounty with feathered friends
by creating a tree full of their favorite winter foods.
Decorate an evergreen tree outside or place a bough cut from
a Christmas tree upright in a window box. Keep a journal
to record the types of birds that visit the tree. You may want
to continue feeding the birds throughout the winter.

Hanging Baskets

Materials Needed

Pencil

12 small paper cups

Red ribbon or string,
2 yards cut into 12 equal pieces

1 pound dried sunflower seeds in shells

1 pound unsalted peanuts, in or out of shells

Fresh cranberries

Apple slices

For each basket, use a pencil to carefully poke 2 holes on opposite sides of the cup, just under the rim. Tie a knot in one end of the yarn or ribbon, then, working from inside the cup, string the ribbon or yarn through one of the holes. String the loose end of the ribbon through the second hole from outside. Tie a knot at the end inside the cup to form a handle.

Mix the seeds, peanuts, cranberries, and apple slices in a bowl, and distribute evenly among the cups. Hang on high branches of a tree, preferably outside a window.

Pinecone Treats

Materials Needed

1 cup natural unsalted peanut butter

1 cup cornmeal

Waxed paper

6 to 8 medium-size pinecones

String or narrow ribbon

Place the peanut butter and cornmeal in the center of a sheet of waxed paper. Mix with a fork until well blended. Roll the pinecones, one at a time, in the mixture until pinecones are well coated. Tie a string around each pinecone in the middle and form a loop. Hang on high branches of a tree or bush.

Outdoor Ice Picture

This is an ideal project for a cold winter day. If you don't have cold weather, you can use a freezer to make a beautiful and temporary ice picture.

Materials Needed

Aluminum pie pan

Water

Cotton string, about 24 inches long

Evergreens, berries, twigs, and leaves, rinsed clean

1. Fill the pie pan with water. Make a loop of string and place it in the pie pan so that about half the loop hangs over the edge (this will be used to hang the ice picture). Submerge the string along the edges of the water.

2. Make an arrangement of evergreen, berries, dried flowers and grasses, twigs, milk pods, moss, or any natural object that you have collected. Set the pie plate outside to freeze overnight, or place in freezer until frozen solid.

3. To remove ice picture, set the base of the pan in warm water (don't get the ice picture wet), and then remove. Hang it outside on a branch near a window. This picture will last as long as the weather is below freezing.

New Year's Eve Piñata

Making a piñata is a perfect way to celebrate the New Year. Fill the decorated piñata with small bags of dried fruit, pieces of wrapped candy, lightweight toys, and holiday doorbells (see page 49). Make a confetti blower for each guest (see page 126) and place inside the piñata. Break open the piñata at any point during the evening.

Material Needed

Sturdy brown paper bag

Markers, stickers, rubber stamps, and streamers

Scissors

String or ribbon, about 3 feet long

Treats such as dried fruit, candy, lightweight toys,
holiday doorbells, and confetti blowers

Tissue paper

Stapler or clear tape

1. Select a sturdy paper shopping bag. The bottom of the bag will become the top of the piñata. Decorate the bag with markers, stickers, streamers, and strips of paper.

2. At the top of the bag, carefully poke a hole on each side using a pencil. Reinforce the edges of each hole with tape. Thread a string through one hole and out the other. Tie the ends of the string together in a knot.

3. Turn the bag upside down and fill it with treats and small toys. Use tissue paper as filler. Fold down the top of the bag twice and staple shut. Hang the piñata and have each guest take turns swinging at it with a plastic baseball bat. When the piñata breaks, share the treats and toys. Happy New Year!

73

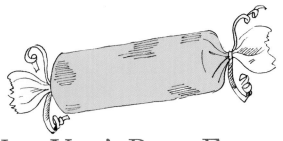

New Year's Party Favors

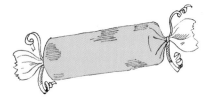

Everybody loves a party favor full of treats. Place on the table at each setting or hand out to each guest before midnight. Fill with paper fortunes, and have each guests read their fortunes aloud for the new year.

Materials Needed

1 empty paper towel tube

Scissors

14-inch square of wrapping or tissue paper (for each favor)

Paper curls, paper fortunes, confetti, candy, chocolate coins, and small trinkets

Glue stick or clear tape

Ribbon

1. Cut the cardboard tube in half. You will need to cut a 14-inch square of paper for each favor. Lay the decorative side of the wrapping paper face down on a flat surface.

2. Fill each tube with paper curls, paper fortunes, confetti, candy, and other party treats. Set the tube at the edge of the paper. Carefully roll the paper over the tube. Glue or tape the edge of the wrapping paper in an even line across the tube.

3. Gently twist the paper at either end, and tie with a colorful ribbon. Use scissors to curl the ends of ribbon.

Valentine Envelope Cards

Make a small handmade envelope and send a secret message for Valentine's Day. Write your message with invisible ink (see page 76). Let the recipient know that to break the code, he or she will need to paint over the message with concentrated red grape juice or food coloring so it will become visible. You can also decorate the envelope with a heart shaped rubber stamp (see page 76).

Materials Needed

3-inch square of your favorite decorative paper

2-inch square of white paper

Invisible ink

1. Rotate the square of decorative paper so it is similar to a diamond shape. Fold in the left and right points toward the center. Crease the edges lightly with your thumb.

2. Fold the bottom point in towards the center so that it overlaps the center of the 2 side folds. To finish, fold the top point down to overlap the other 3 points. Crease along the fold with your thumb to make an envelope.

3. Write your message on a 2-inch square sheet of white paper. Place it in the envelope. Seal the envelope with a decorative sticker or a piece of tape.

Extra Ideas: Square and heart-shaped paper doilies can be used for a valentine envelope cards.

Invisible Ink

Materials Needed

Water

Baking soda

Cotton swab or small paintbrush

Red grape juice concentrate, thawed (for viewing)

In a small bowl, mix equal parts water and baking soda. Use the baking soda solution as "ink" and write a message onto white paper, using a cotton swab or paintbrush. Let the message dry before enclosing it in an envelope. To reveal the message, paint over it with grape juice concentrate.

Rubber Stamp Hearts

Materials Needed

Pen

Gum eraser

Craft knife

Red ink pad or watercolor

1. Using a pen, draw a large heart onto the eraser's surface. **With Adult Help,** use a craft knife to carefully cut into the side of the eraser. Cut around the outer edges of the heart shape until all excess portions have been removed, leaving only the heart-shaped design.

2. Test the stamp by pressing onto an ink pad, and then onto a sheet of paper. If necessary, carve away more of the eraser to create the desired shape.

Quick-Thinking Valentines

*Sometimes we just have to hurry to make our valentines,
especially if it is on a school night. Here are a few simple ideas that
will have everyone asking who made this great valentine.*

Use a heart-shaped cookie cutter as a template and trace the shape onto
decorative paper. Trace a smaller heart on white tissue paper. Cut out heart and
paste the smaller heart on top of the larger heart. Write your valentine a silly
rhyme and sign it "Guess Who?"

Take an old piece of decorative fabric and cut it in the shape of a heart.
You can use whatever is available—it could be heavy upholstery fabric,
a worn-out cloth bag, or a piece of felt or lace. Glue the fabric onto a
similarly shaped piece of cardboard or poster board. Next, cut and glue a
paper heart made of heavy construction paper or card stock onto the fabric
heart. Glue beads and sequins along the edges. Make beaded dangle strings
(see page 121) for the edges if you have time. Write a valentine message on
the heart with rubber stamps, invisible ink (see page 76), or watercolor paints.
Place the valentine in an envelope or wrap it in tissue paper. Decorate it with
candy hearts.

Valentine Carrier

Take an old shoebox and slice a slot in the lid. Cover
with aluminum foil. Cut out heart shapes made of
colored foil (from candy wrappers or foil from the craft
stores). Paste paper heart shapes or an old valentine on
the top. Make it fun and different!

Spring

Spring Projects

March

Kites That Really Fly

Kite-Flying Tips

Paper Sled Kite

Two-Stick Diamond Kite

May

Rose Petal Beads

Rose Water

Homemade Soap

Mother's Day Potato Print Card

Handmade Paper

Accordian Fold-Out Cards

Tussie-Mussie

Language of Flowers

Papier-Mâché Pins

Simple Sewing

Needle Case

April

Coloring Eggs

Natural Dyes

Blowing Eggs

Sponge-Painted Eggs

Eggshell Garden

80

Kites That Really Fly

Kites are a very old invention. In ancient China, kites were flown as a way to send messages to the gods. The paintings on kites were the message: a dragon for wealth, a bird for peace or good luck, as well as many others. Kites have also been used scientifically as a tool to understand the weather patterns. Best of all, flying a kite is fun. You may want to experiment with the size of the kite and the weight of the paper to see which works best.

Kite-Flying Tips

• Never fly a kite in rain or lightning. Electricity in clouds is attracted to damp kite lines and kite fliers.

• Fly your kite in an open area on a windy day. Open fields, parks, and beaches are the best places for kiting. Avoid areas where the kite could get tangled up in tree branches and on telephone wires.

• Try flying your kite in a medium wind. A medium wind is one that moves leaves and bushes lightly.

• Be sure to add a cloth tail. A lightweight tail helps to keep the kite's nose pointing into the wind.

• You can make your kite dance by pulling in the line and letting it out slowly.

Paper Sled Kite

*Sled kites are known to be flexible flyers because they change their form
with the wind. Make one using a lightweight brown paper bag or a plastic
shopping bag. Your kite can be any size, large or very small, but always start with
a square shape and follow this method for sizing the kite.*

Materials Needed

18-inch square lightweight paper (for the sail)

Scissors

Ruler

Pencil

2 wooden dowels, ¼ inch by 18 inches long

Duct tape or clear packing tape

String for bridle, about 20 inches long

String for flying, about 10 feet long

Stick or twig, for string winder

3 strips of 2-by-24-inch lightweight cloth or ribbon for tails

1. Measure and cut an 18-inch square of lightweight paper. Fold the square in half lengthwise, and then fold in half again. Open paper to original size. You will have 4 equal panels (Fig. 1)

2. Next measure 6 inches down or ⅓ of the total, from the top on both sides of the center fold and mark a point with your pencil. Using your ruler, draw a line across to connect the 2 points. These are the A-B points on the kite (Fig 2).

3. To make the kite shape, draw a cutting line across each corner from A-B points on sides to x points on top and y points on the bottom as shown in red (Fig. 2). Cut from point to point to make your sled kite shape.

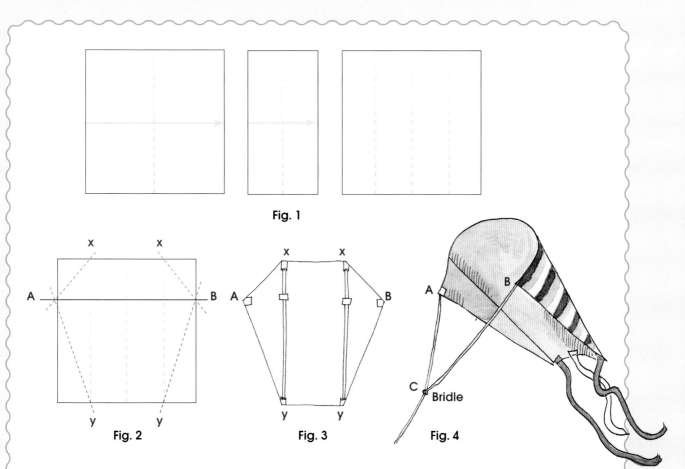

Fig. 1

Fig. 2

Fig. 3

Fig. 4

Bridle

4. Cut 2 wooden dowels, each 18 inches long. Tape the dowels firmly to points x and y at the top and bottom, and along the A-B line in the middle. Reinforce the outside A-B points with tape (Fig. 3).

5. Cut a 20-inch length of string for the bridle. Tape one end of the bridle string to point A and one to point B (Fig. 4).

6. Cut a piece of string about 10 feet long. Tie one end of the flying string to the middle of the bridle, at point C (Fig. 4). Wrap the rest of the string around the small twig or stick. This will be the handle and string winder. Use tape to attach the kite tails firmly to the bottom of the kite. Fly your kite outside on a moderately windy day.

Two-Stick Diamond Kite

This classic kite takes a little extra time to construct, but it flies like a champion.

Materials Needed

2 wooden dowels, ¼ inch by 30 inches and 36 inches long

Scissors

String

Glue

Screwdriver or craft knife

Lightweight paper or plastic (for the sail),
about 32 by 38 inches

Duct tape or clear packing tape

String for bridle, about 40 inches long

String for tail, about 36 inches long

6 strips of 2-by-8-inch lightweight cloth or ribbon for tail

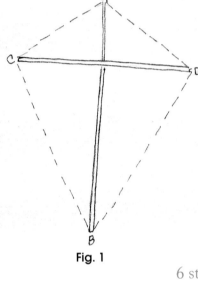

Fig. 1

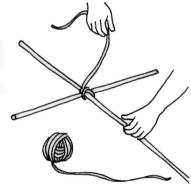

Fig. 2

1. Cut dowel A-B 36 inches long. Cut dowel C-D 30 inches long. Make a cross with the two dowels (Fig. 1). Place the shorter one horizontally across the longer stick. Make sure the cross piece is centered so that each side is the same. Tie the two sticks together with the string, and dab glue to reinforce the joint (Fig. 2). Let the glue dry.

2. With Adult Help, cut a notch with a screwdriver or knife at each end of both sticks (Fig. 3). Make the notches deep enough to fit the string into them securely. This will keep the string in place on the stick as you wrap.

3. Cut a piece of string long enough to stretch all around the kite frame. Make a loop in the top notch, and fasten it by wrapping the string around the stick. Wrap string around each of these notches to form an outline of the kite. Finish wrapping the string around the top stick and tie at the top. Cut off the extra string. This string frame must be taut but not so tight as to warp or bend the sticks.

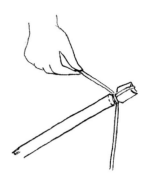

Fig. 3

4. Lay the sail material flat and place the stick frame face down on top. Cut around the string outline, leaving about a 1-inch margin all around (Fig. 4). Fold these edges over the string frame, and tape or glue it down so that the material is tight. Wrap the remaining string around a stick or firm twig.

5. Cut a piece of string about 40 inches long, and fasten it to points C and D to make the bridle. Tie your long flying string to the center of the bridle string.

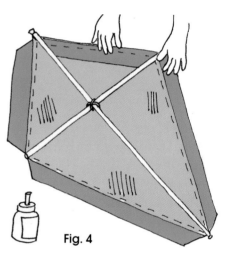

Fig. 4

6. Make a long tail by cutting a piece of string about 36 inches long, and tie on 3 to 4 strips of cloth or ribbon every 6 inches along the string. Attach the tail to the bottom of your kite with strong tape, then go outside and fly it!

The Easter Egg

*The best colored eggs need to be perfectly hard-cooked, so that there are no cracks in the shell. Put eggs in a large pot, in a single layer and cover them with cold water. **With Adult Help**, turn on the heat and bring the water to a full boil. Remove the pan from the heat and allow the eggs to sit in the hot water for about 15 to 20 minutes. Run cold water over the eggs until completely cooled, then refrigerate until ready to use.*

Coloring Eggs

Coloring eggs was part of a spring tradition in early Europe. It is said that eggs were buried when the fields were plowed or hung from fruit trees to ensure a good harvest. Make your own tribute to spring and Easter by coloring and decorating eggs in a variety of ways.

Materials Needed

Newspapers

Empty egg carton

Water

Bowls, plastic containers, or mugs

White vinegar

Liquid food coloring

Spoons

Empty egg carton for drying eggs

1. Cover work area with plenty of newspaper. Turn empty egg carton upside down on paper to use as a drying rack.

2. With Adult Help, bring 3 to 6 cups of water to a boil and remove from heat. Add 1 tablespoon of white vinegar and 3 to 4 drops of liquid food coloring per cup.

3. Decorate the eggs using a variety of methods; draw designs with crayons, wrap rubber bands in patterns around eggs, or cover with stickers to make polka dot eggs.

4. Place hard-cooked egg in bowl with dye. Use a spoon to coat the eggs with dye. Soak the eggs in dye for 1 to 2 minutes for a lighter color and longer for a deeper, richer color. Remove each egg with a spoon and place it on an upside-down egg carton to dry. Take off rubber bands and stickers when the eggs dry.

Natural Dyes

*Try coloring eggs using everyday foods that are found in the kitchen. **With Adult Help**, prepare the dyes in advance. Some ingredients require boiling the vegetables or fruit. Soak the eggs in about 1 cup of prepared liquid dye. Natural dyes will give you a softer color than store-bought food coloring.*

Red: Beets, boiled or juice from pickled beets, cranberries, frozen strawberries

Orange: Yellow onion skins, boiled

Pale green: Spinach leaves, boiled

Green-gold: Yellow Delicious apple peels, boiled

Blue: Canned blueberries, red cabbage leaves, boiled

Beige to brown: Strong brewed coffee or boiled walnut shells

Purple: Grape juice

Yellow: Ground turmeric powder, boiled

Blowing Eggs

Blowing eggs involves blowing out the contents of a raw egg into a bowl. When colored and stored properly, they can last for years. Make several batches until you have a unique collection of decorative eggs. Display in a decorative berry basket or a festive bowl filled with paper grass.

Materials Needed

Newspapers

Eggs

Needle or paperclip

Bowl

Empty egg carton for drying eggs

1. Clean the outside of the eggs with soapy water and dry well with towel. Using a needle or a paper clip, poke a small hole in the narrow end of the egg, and a slightly larger hole in the other end. Move the pin around inside the egg to loosen the inside of the egg.

2. Over a bowl, blow through the smaller hole to force the contents out of the larger opening. Rinse the egg and allow it to dry on an egg carton before painting or dyeing. *Be sure to always wash your hands with warm soapy water after handling raw eggs.*

Sponge-Painted Eggs

Colored eggs don't always have to be dipped and dyed.
Try using sponged-on paint to make speckled eggs. Use a variety of
sponges with different-size holes. Add layers of colors or make
a simple pattern by using one color.

Materials Needed

Hard-cooked eggs

Tempera or watercolor paints

Sponge

Paper plate

Paper towel

Empty egg carton for drying eggs

1. Cut sponge into small squares, one for each color. Add small amounts of different colors of paint to a paper plate. Hold an egg in your fingers, and dab a sponge into desired paint color with the other hand. Dab the sponge onto a piece of paper towel to absorb extra paint. Sponge directly onto your egg and make a pattern on the top half and sides.

2. Set the egg on top of an empty egg carton to dry. When the paint is dry, complete painting the bottom of the egg and allow that to dry as well. Place your eggs in a bowl or berry basket filled with paper grass.

Eggshell Garden

*Celebrate the coming of spring by planting seeds
in decorative eggshells and watching the seedlings grow!
Use fast-growing grass seeds, or plant spring flowers
and herbs that are found in plant stores.*

Materials Needed

6 large eggs

Spoons

Small bowls

Dish towel

Empty egg carton

Aluminum foil

Egg dyes

Potting soil

Grass or flower seeds

1. Gently tap the pointed end of an uncooked egg with the edge of the spoon until you have cracked the egg top to about the size of a quarter. Remove the chipped shell, and gently shake the contents of the egg into the bowl. When you're done, set the bowl in refrigerator. Use later to make scrambled eggs if you like. *Be sure to wash your hands with warm soapy water after handling raw eggs.*

2. Carefully wash the inside and the outside of each shell with warm soapy water and set on a dish towel to dry.

3. Set out a series of bowls for egg dyeing (see page 86). You will need 1 bowl per color. Dip each egg in dye, then place it on an empty egg carton to dry.

4. Line each section of empty egg carton with aluminum foil. This allows the eggshell to stand upright in the carton. Place eggshells in the lined sections. Fill each eggshell halfway with potting soil. Add a pinch of grass or flower seeds and mix lightly into the soil with a spoon or your finger.

5. Water well and cover with newspaper or a clean dish towel, and place near a sunny window. Water lightly every day for 1 week. After a week small sprouts of plants will appear. Uncover and continue to water the plants occasionally. Keep them in a sunny room.

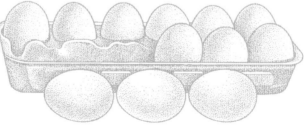

Extra Ideas: Paint and decorate an empty cardboard egg carton using poster paint, or wrap the carton in aluminum foil, and decorate it with markers.

Rose Petal Beads

*Use rose petals to make special Mother's Day gifts. If you can,
use very fragrant petals for this project. If you don't have a rose
garden, ask a neighbor or a local florist for some extra petals.*

Materials Needed

Fresh rose petals, about 5 cups

Water

Rose essential oil

Wooden spoon or spatula

Blender

Toothpicks

1. Collect 5 cups of the most fragrant rose petals from a garden.
Discard any old and wilted petals. Add ¼ cup of water and
2 cups of petals to blender and place lid on securely. Chop the
mixture until the paste is fine and like clay. Transfer the paste to
a bowl. Blend the remaining petals with 2 tablespoons of water
for each cup of petals. If the pulp is too watery, then pat the pulp
with a paper towel or sponge to absorb extra water.

2. Place a drop of rose oil on your fingertips. Roll a small amount
of paste in the palm of your hand to form a bead about the size
of a large marble. Poke a toothpick through the center of each
bead to form a hole, leaving the toothpicks in the beads. Allow
the beads to dry for 3 to 5 days, or until they harden.

3. Remove the toothpicks and allow the beads to dry for 2 more days. String beads on heavy embroidery thread to make a necklace or a bracelet. Store in a jar filled with cotton balls dipped in rose oil.

Rose Water

Make homemade perfume using fresh rose petals.
Try to use fragrant petals for this project.

Materials Needed

Fresh rose petals, about 1 cup

2 cups of spring water

Heat-resistant glass bowl and cover

Cheesecloth, cotton gauze, or kitchen strainer

Glass jar

1. Gather one packed cup of rose petals. Place in heat-resistant bowl. **With Adult Help**, add boiling water.

2. Cover the bowl and let it sit for 30 minutes. Strain the petals and water mixture through cheesecloth into a clean lidded jar or misting bottle. Discard the rose petals or save to make rose beads (see page 92). Refrigerate for up to 3 weeks.

Homemade Soap

This is a perfect gift for moms and grandmothers who love soap and clean hands. Make a batch of scented soap for Mother's Day or just swirl in some colors to make an unscented batch of clean fun. Glycerin and scented oils can be found at most craft stores.

Materials Needed

Newspapers

1 empty half-gallon milk or juice carton,
to use as a mold

Knife

Double boiler

1 lb. clear glycerin, to make 4 to 5 bars of soap

Wooden coffee stirrers

Essential oil (optional)

1. Cover your work surface with newspapers. Open the top of a milk or juice carton completely (you should have 4 straight sides). Clean and dry the inside of the carton and set aside.

2. **With Adult Help**, cut the glycerin into small pieces with a sharp knife. Place the glycerin blocks in the top pan of a double boiler. Add about 1 cup of water in the base of the double boiler and bring it to a boil. Turn the heat to low, and place the top pan over the water. Stir occasionally until the glycerin is completely melted.

3. If desired, add 2 to 4 drops of scented oil and stir with a wooden stirrer until it is well mixed.

4. Using a pot holder, pour the melted glycerin from the pan into the carton. Let it cool completely (about 2 hours). When it is cool, tear away the carton. **With Adult Help,** use a knife to slice the block into 4 to 5 individual bars.

Extra Ideas: Make swirly colored soap bars by adding several drops of food coloring to the melted glycerin. Swirl colors with a wooden stirrer.

Wrap the bars in waxed paper and tie them with colorful twine or raffia and give as gifts.

Mother's Day Potato Print Card

Materials Needed

Paper, blank white or colored paper, any size

Paring knife

Pencil

3 large baking potatoes

Tempera paints

Paper plate for each color, to hold paint

Pens or markers

Glue

1. Fold a piece of paper in half to make a card shape you like.

2. With Adult Help, cut each potato in half widthwise. The raw surface of the potatoes will be used as the stamp for your prints.

3. Draw several favorite shapes on paper that can be used for the stamp designs. Some good shapes to try are stars, circles, triangles, and hearts. You can also draw the letters MOM.

4. Cut out the shapes and trace them onto the raw surface of the potatoes. Then, use the paring knife to carve away the background.

5. Pour each color of paint into the saucers. Dip the potato stamps into the paint and press them onto the paper. Decorate the front, back, or inside of the card to your liking. Glue flowers or sequins to the card to make it extra special. Write a poem or special note in your best handwriting for mom or grandmother.

Handmade Paper

You can make handmade paper by using a rotary beater, recycled paper, a screened wooden frame, and water. Buy a wooden frame from a craft store or make one yourself. Be prepared to get a little wet. Once you have sheets of beautiful one-of-a-kind paper, make handmade cards and valentines (see page 77), or a tussie-mussie (see page 102) for yourself and as gifts. If you don't like the result of the paper, tear it up and recycle it for the next project.

Materials Needed

2 wooden frames, about 8 by 10 inches

Screen, about 7 ½ by 9 ½ inches

Stapler

Brown paper grocery bag,
watercolor paper (or an old watercolor painting
that you want to recycle), and/or tissue paper

Plastic bucket (for soaking torn paper pieces)

Large sheet of plastic for a table covering

Measuring cup

Large pan (for blending pulp)

Rotary beater

Large plastic dishpan (for dipping)

3 to 4 cotton dish towels

Sponge

1. Buy or make two wooden frames about 8 by 10 inches. Staple the screen to one of the frames to make a mold (Fig. 1). The other frame, the deckle, sits on top of the screened frame. The deckle will contain the pulp within the surface of the screen. The deckle frame determines how large your sheet will be. Stack the deckle on top of the screened frame and set aside.

Fig. 1

2. To make the pulp, tear a brown bag and watercolor paper into small pieces. Place the pieces in a large plastic bucket and soak in water overnight.

3. When you are ready to blend the pulp, lay a plastic sheet over your work surface to protect it. Place about 1 cup of soaked paper and 2 cups of water in a large pan. Beat the mixture with a rotary beater until the paper is smooth and liquid (Fig 2). Continue to beat the pulp a little longer if there are big chunks of paper in it.

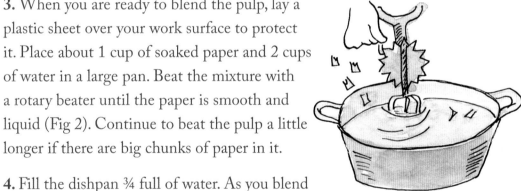

Fig. 2

4. Fill the dishpan ¾ full of water. As you blend the paper, pour each batch into the dishpan. Repeat until all of the soaked paper has been blended and added to the tub. Add flowers and grasses to the water, if desired. They will float in the water and become part of the paper sheet.

5. Make a padding of dish towels on a work surface near the dishpan. Use a spoon or your hands to swirl the water to make all of the pulp float in the water. Lower the stacked frames into the dishpan at an angle (Fig. 3), and set them on the bottom of the tub. The screened frame will collect the pulp in a thick layer. The top frame (deckle) will help mold the shape of the paper. Hold the frames on both sides and quickly lift it straight up (Fig. 4).

Fig. 3

Fig. 4

6. Hold the frames over the dishpan and drain well. Bring the frames to the pad of towels and turn upside down in the center of the towels. Lift off the screens, leaving the paper sheet on the towel (Fig. 5).

Fig. 5

Fig. 6

7. Blot the paper gently with a paper towel or sponge to absorb extra water. Lift the paper sheet up and set it on a flat surface to dry completely (Fig. 6). Repeat until all of the pulp in the dishpan has been used.

Accordion Fold-Out Cards

Once you learn how to make a fold-out card, you can use the format to make any type of card. Add pressed flowers and write a poem to create a birthday card. Cut pictures and words for each panel to make a story or invitation. Be sure to decorate both sides of the panels.

Materials Needed

1 sheet of handmade paper, about 7 ½ by 9½ inches

Pencil

Ruler

Glue

2 lengths of thin ribbon, about 12 inches long

Paper punch

1. Fold a sheet of paper in half widthwise. Crease well with edge of ruler.

2. Fold each edge back to the original fold. Crease well and open. You will have 4 panels.

3. Punch a hole in the middle of each outer panel. Tie a thin ribbon through each hole. After decorating the inside of the card, fold up card, tie and give as a special gift.

Extra Ideas: Use pressed flowers to decorate the front and inside of a card. Take each flower and carefully brush glue on one side. Place the flower onto the paper and press lightly. Create a circle design in the center of the card, or arrange the flowers throughout the card in a way that you like.

Paste a favorite picture or poem on each panel. You can also glue leaves and small twigs on the card. Make letters using leaves and twigs to spell out HAPPY BIRTHDAY or BEST FRIENDS.

Tussie-Mussie

A tussie-mussie is a small bunch of sweet scented flowers, set into a paper cone shape. The traditional tussie-mussie is filled with fragrant herbs surrounding one central flower, a rose. Make a tussie-mussie with freshly molded handmade paper (see page 98) for moms, dads, grandparents, and teachers.

Materials Needed

5-inch square of construction paper

Scissors

Stapler

6-inch sheet handmade paper

Dish towel

Fresh or dried flowers

1. Cut a piece of construction paper into a square. Position the square in a diamond shape. Then wrap the left corner over the right, to form a cone shape. Staple the top overlap and the bottom point.

2. Make a sheet of handmade paper using the paper-making method (see page 98). Add extra flowers and grasses to the pulp to make it decorative.

3. After pulling the sheet from the mold, wrap the wet paper around the cone. Press the edges of the wet paper against the cone. The damp paper will allow you to shape it around the cone.

4. Fill the cone with herbs or flowers. Create a message with flowers using the flower chart (see page 103).

Language of Flowers

Flowers were once used as a secret language to express love, friendship, and sorrow. This flower chart shows some of the meanings for flowers. Make a tussie-mussie for someone special and use the flower chart to express your own message.

Basil, *Love*
Baby's Breath, *Pure heart*
Carnation, *Admiration*
Chrysanthemum, *Cheerfulness*
Daisy, *Innocence*
Fern, *Sincerity*
Ivy, *Fidelity, friendship, marriage*
Jasmine, *Grace*
Johnny Jump Up, *Happy thoughts*
Lavender Luck, *Devotion*
Lemon Balm, *Sympathy*
Lily, *Modesty*
Lily of the Valley, *Purity*
Marigold, *Grief*
Marjoram, *Kindness, courtesy*
Mint, *Warm feelings*
Oregano, *Joy*
Pansy, *Loving thoughts*

Periwinkle, *Happy memory*
Red Poppy, *Consolation*
Rose, red, *Love*
Rose, pink, *Grace, beauty*
Rose, yellow, *Friendship*
Rosemary, *Remembrance*
Sage, *Wisdom*
Snowdrop, *Hope*
Star of Bethlehem, *Purity*
Sweet Pea, *Departure, tender memory*
Sweet William, *Gallantry*
Tulip, red, *Renewed love*
Violet, *Loyalty, modesty, humility*
Violet, blue, *Faithfulness*
Wheat, *Good fortune*
Weeping willow, *Mourning*
Zinnia, *Thoughts of friends far away*

Papier-Mâché Pins

Animal pins are special and simple gifts to make for Mother's Day or for your own collection of pins. Decorate with paints and beads, or keep it a simple color. You can buy pin backs at craft stores.

Materials Needed

Pencil

Tracing paper

Cardboard

White glue, diluted

Strips of newspaper

Paintbrush

Tempera paints (for children)

Sandpaper

Glue

Pin back (1 per pin)

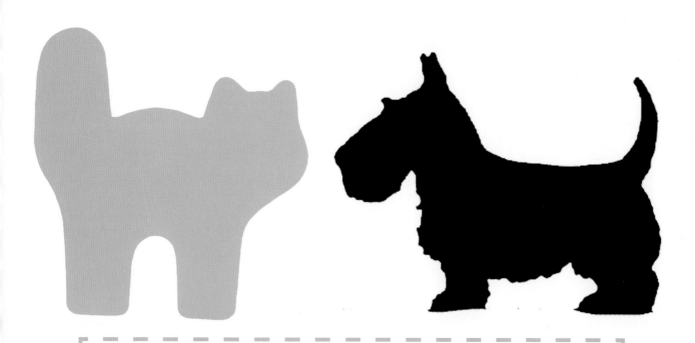

1. Trace the cat or dog template above or draw your own favorite animal shape. Transfer the shape onto the cardboard and use scissors cut it out.

2. Fill a small bowl with glue. Using a paintbrush, stir in warm water and mix until glue is thin but not watery. Add a little more glue if it needs to be thickened.

3. Dip several strips of newspaper into the paste and wrap three layers around the cut-out shape. Be sure to cover all of the cardboard with newspaper strips. Allow to it to dry overnight.

4. When the paper is completely dry, smooth the surface with a fine piece of sandpaper. Brush a coat of white paint on the surface of the paper. Paint one or two more coats, if necessary, to cover all traces of the newspaper print. Let it dry, about 1 hour.

5. Paint in details, as desired. You can paint stripes, dots, and patterns or keep it a simple color. Make a collar from paint or beads. Glue the pin back to the back of the shape. Let it dry overnight.

Simple Sewing

The up-and-down straight stitch is an easy one for beginning crafters to master. Use it to sew two pieces of fabric together or to embroider a small decorative flower on fabric.

1. To begin, measure out a length of thread about 10 inches long. Moisten the tip of the thread to a point, and then poke it through the eye of a needle. Pull the thread through the needle about 3 inches. This will help prevent the thread from slipping out. Tie a knot at the base of the thread tail.

2. To practice the up-and-down stitch poke threaded needle up through the underside of the fabric, and pull until the knot tugs up against it (Fig. 1).

3. Next, poke the needle down along the seam line (Fig. 2). Pull the needle down through the fabric, and then poke it up to where the next stitch will start, then poke down through, and up until you have reached the end of the seam (Fig. 3). When you finish your seam, tie a knot as close to underside of the fabric as possible. This knot prevents the thread from slipping through and unraveling.

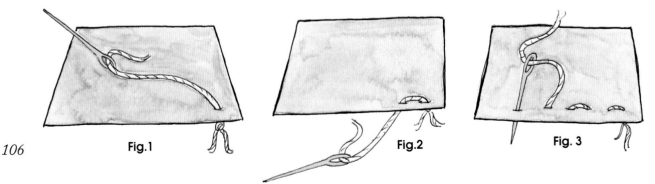

Fig.1   Fig.2   Fig. 3

Needle Case

This needle case is a perfect and practical first sewing project. It also makes a wonderful Mother's Day gift.

Materials Needed

Tracing paper

Colored felt

Flannel or cotton fabric

Pencil or chalk

Large-eyed needle

Thread

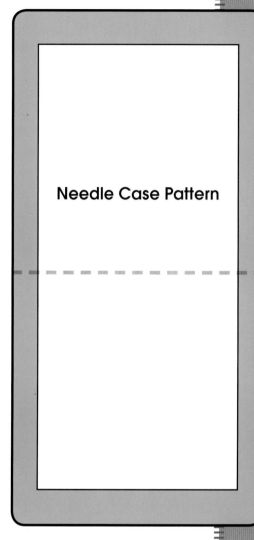

Needle Case Pattern

1. Trace the blue outline of the pattern on tracing paper and cut it out. Lay the pattern on top of a piece of colored felt and cut out the same shape.

2. Cut a piece of flannel to match the white outline of your pattern. It will be a little smaller than the felt piece. Fold the flannel along the middle dotted line as shown on the pattern. Center the flannel inside the felt piece as shown.

3. To stitch the two pieces of fabric together, use a pencil or chalk to mark a dotted line as shown in the pattern. Thread a needle and sew along the dotted line using the up-and-down stitch (see page 106). When you're finished, tie a knot at the end of the string. Fold the case in half. Store pins and needles on the inside flannel flap. Keep the case in your sewing basket.

Extra Ideas: Trace a flower on the outside front flap. Embroider along the outline using the up-and-down stitch and embroidery thread.

Summer

Summer Projects

June

Firefly Lantern
Spider Web Collecting
Pressed Flowers
Daisy Chain
Dandelion Bracelet
Make a Wish
U.S. State Flower Chart
Collecting State Flowers
Paper Glider
Parachute
Quick Slingshot
Pinwheel
Dangle Bead Bookmark
Big Bubbles
Bubble Wands
Bubble Cone
Bubble Art

July

Five-Pointed Star
4th of July Confetti Blower
Paper Hat
Quill Pen
Feather Collecting
Feather Journal
Directions
Magnetic Compass
Paper Drinking Cup
Seashell Candles
Treasure Jar

August

Summer Travel Scrapbook
More Fun with Scrapbooks
Drawstring Field Bag
Animal Track Casting
Campfire Stories
Toasting Marshmallows
Back-Yard Camping

Firefly Lantern
(Catch and Release)

Materials Needed

Glass or plastic jar with lid

Summer evening

June evenings are the best time to observe fireflies dancing in the meadows. Gently catch a blinking firefly by cupping your hands over it in midair.

Carefully slide each firefly into the jar and replace the lid. Your jar will become a lantern and glow from the light of the fireflies.

After observing these living lanterns, open the jar lid and release the fireflies back into their natural habitat.

Extra Ideas: U.S. fireflies that blink are not typically found west of the state of Kansas.

Spider Web Collecting

Collecting spider webs can be fun and educational. These intricate geometric constructions provide hours of observation. Be sure to collect spider webs when the weavers are away. If there is a spider in the web, gently scare it away with a twig. The spider will go off to create a new web elsewhere. Do not touch or harm a spider.

Materials Needed

Non-toxic white enamel spray paint

Newspaper (to protect plants)

A sheet of multicolored construction
paper for each web

1. Once you locate an empty spider web, place newspapers around the area where you will be spraying paint. This helps protect other plants in the garden from getting sprayed.

2. Carefully spray both sides of the web with a small amount of paint. Spray the paint in quick bursts to prevent the web from breaking.

3. When the web is fully coated with paint, set a sheet of construction paper underneath or against one side of the web (whichever is easiest to reach without breaking the web). Carefully press the sheet of paper to the sticky web. Try to move smoothly and evenly as you catch the web. Allow the web to adhere firmly to the paper before moving it. Set the mounted web aside to dry.

Collecting and drying garden flowers and wildflowers is a great hobby. It's a wonderful way to study flowers and foliage available in your area and to learn the basics of plant classification. Once you have a collection of dried flowers, you may want to use extras to create original greeting cards, bookmarks, and journals. Make sure you pick your flowers at their freshest, and press when there is no moisture on them.

Pressed Flowers

Here are a few tips for pressing flowers at home using simple materials.

Materials Needed

Fresh flowers

Newspaper or construction paper

Large book or old telephone book

1. Pick your favorite flowers. Violets, daisies, Queen Anne's lace, clover, or any garden flower will make pretty arrangements when pressed. Place them in the refrigerator in a container filled with water until ready to use. Use a paper towel to pat any excess moisture from the stems before pressing.

2. When preparing a flower for pressing, consider how it will look when flattened. Leaves should be laid out flat to resemble the natural shape of the flower.

3. Place the flowers or foliage on the inside fold of the sheet of newspaper or between 2 sheets of construction paper. When you are pleased with your arrangement, fold the top half of the newspaper sheet down over the flowers. If you are using construction paper, place a second sheet of paper on top of the arrangement.

4. Carefully place a large book on top of the paper, making sure that the area with the flower is completely covered. A dictionary, encyclopedia, or telephone book works well. The drying process takes about 3 days.

5. Once the flowers are pressed and dried, store your flower collection in a homemade scrapbook (see page 134). Pressed flowers can also be glued to accordion fold-out cards (see page 101), bookmarks, and wooden frames to make unique gifts.

Daisy Chain

Make a friendship necklace using only daisies. Your grandparent may remember this craft from their childhood. Make one for your grandparent or an elderly friend as a summer gift. Daisies usually bloom in late spring and early summer. For best results, pick daisies with long, thick stems.

Materials Needed

12 to 15 daisies with long, thick stems

1. Pick daisies, one at a time. Use your thumbnail to split the stalk of one of the daisies about halfway down its length. It will make an opening or a loop in the middle of the stem.

2. Thread the stalk of another daisy through this opening, then to make another opening in the next daisy stalk with your thumbnail. Continue to thread until you have a necklace length you like. Tie the end of the last stem to the base of the first daisy. Be sure to make the necklace long enough to go over your head easily after it has been tied.

Dandelion Bracelet

*If you find yourself lazing around in the yard one
summer day, try picking some dandelions and make
a friendship bracelet. Give it to your best friend.*

Materials Needed

5 to 6 long-stemmed dandelions

Attach the dandelions to one another by tying the stem
in a knot around the stem of another dandelion. Tie it as
close to the base of the flower as possible. Continue to tie
stems together until you have a length that you like. Tie
the ends of the final two stems in a double knot and slip
it on. Make another for a friend.

Make a Wish

A dandelion flower will eventually
turn into a puffy globe. Blowing the
seeds off a dandelion globe is said to
carry your thoughts and dreams to
your loved one. Make a wish and let
the wind carry it away.

U.S. State Flower Chart

Alabama, Camellia

Alaska, Forget-me-not

Arizona, Saguaro cactus

Arkansas, Apple blossom

California, California poppy

Colorado, Rocky mountain

Connecticut, Mountain laurel

Delaware, Peach blossom

Florida, Orange blossom

Georgia, Cherokee rose

Hawaii, Pua aloalo

Idaho, Syringa

Illinois, Purple violet

Indiana, Peony

Iowa, Wild prairie rose

Kansas, Sunflower

Kentucky, Goldenrod

Louisiana, Magnolia

Maine, White pinecone and tassel

Maryland, Black-eyed susan

Massachusetts, Trailing arbutus

Michigan, Apple blossom

Minnesota, Pink and white lady's slipper

Mississippi, Magnolia

Missouri, Hawthorn

Montana, Bitterroot

Nebraska, Goldenrod

Nevada, Sagebrush

New Hampshire, Purple lilac

New Jersey, Violet

New Mexico, Yucca flower

New York, Rose

North Carolina, American dogwood

North Dakota, Wild prairie rose

Ohio, Scarlet carnation

Oklahoma, Mistletoe

Oregon, Oregon grape

Pennsylvania, Mountain laurel

Rhode Island, Violet

South Carolina, Yellow jessamine

South Dakota, Pasque flower

Tennessee, Iris

Texas, Bluebonnet

Utah, Sego lily

Vermont, Red clover

Virginia, American dogwood

Washington, Coast rhododendron

West Virginia, Rhododendron

Wisconsin, Wood violet

Wyoming, Indian paintbrush

Collecting State Flowers

Collecting state flowers is a great way to learn about plant species. It's also a fun way to brush up on state names. Each of the 50 states and several United States territories have an official tree and flower. If you can't find the flower in your area, have a friend or relative in another state send you a postcard with their state flower on it for your scrapbook collection.

Make a scrapbook (see page 134) to organize your state flower collection, or use a three-ring binder. Alphabetize the flowers by state. Decorate the pages with pictures and facts that you have collected. You can organize your collection by gluing the back of mailing envelopes to the pages. Label and store pressed flowers (see page 113) inside each envelope.

Extra Ideas: Collect seed packets or pictures for every state flower in the United States. Tape the packet or picture in your scrapbook, and label it with a note about its origin. For each state flower ask, when did it become the state flower, and why was it chosen? Are there any special stories or myths about the flower? Use the seeds to plants a state flower garden in your back yard. Cut and press the flowers for your scrapbook.

Paper Glider

This simple glider is easy to make, and it really works! It will glide far and wide indoors or out. Decorate it with stickers or markers, and give it name.
Have a contest with friends to see whose can fly the best. Experiment with other types of paper planes once you've mastered this plane.

Materials Needed

1 sheet of 8 ½-by-11-inch paper

Paperclip

1. Fold the paper in half lengthwise and press firmly to crease. Open up the paper. Fold down each top corner at one end to meet the inside crease line in the middle. Refold along the outside crease line with the folded corners facing in.

2. Fold back each outer edge to meet the outside crease line. Press each crease firmly after folding. Fold back the edges again so the sides meet.

3. Adjust the wings to open out—like an airplane. Fasten a paperclip toward the front of the plane to help it balance in flight. Toss your plane into the air, and watch it loop and glide.

Extra Ideas: Paper glider experts recommend flicking your wrist gently to make the plane fly. This allows the glider to take it own course. If you hurl it, the glider may crash to the ground.

Parachute

Make a parachute and watch it float through the air. Make several with friends, and have a contest to see whose can float the longest.
Try tossing your parachute from a high place, but be careful not to climb in areas that an adult hasn't approved of.

Materials Needed

1 lightweight cotton handkerchief or paper napkin

4 lengths of lightweight string, about 12 inches long

Bottle cork

Cut 4 lengths of string about 12 inches long. Tie one end of each string around each corner of the handkerchief or paper napkin. Then, tie the other end of each string around the cork. Fold up the parachute and toss in the air.

Extra Ideas: You can also use a clothespin for your parachute. Tie the ends of the string around the top of pin and toss it in the air.

Quick Slingshot

1. Find a sturdy, Y-shaped branch about 6 to 9 inches long that is already dried. Cut a long, thick rubber band in half. Cut a rectangular piece of strong cloth (such as denim) about 2 by 4 inches. Using scissors, cut a slit on each short side of the fabric. The slits should be parallel to the edges, and just large enough for the rubber band to fit through.

2. For each side, slip one end of the rubber band through the slit, and tie a double knot. Attach each loose end of the rubber band to the top of each stick, then tie in double knot. Place the folded-up parachute in the slingshot pocket and send it skyward. Try to make it go as high as possible.

Pinwheel

Pinwheels are wonderful wind machines. You can vary the size of your pinwheel, but always use a square piece of paper. Hold your pinwheel against the wind, or blow on it to make it spin.

Materials Needed

6-inch square of lightweight decorative
or origami paper

Pencil

Scissors

Glue

Pushpin

Wooden dowel or wooden chopstick

1. Fold paper in half diagonally, then fold in half again, pressing the crease of the paper lightly with the tips of your fingers. Unfold the paper. Cut along each crease about two-thirds of the way to the square's center. Working clockwise, bend one corner into the center of the pinwheel. Add a dab of glue and press down firmly to secure the paper. Let the glue dry for a few minutes, and continue to overlap each point in the center.

2. To attach the pinwheel to the stick, place the back of the pinwheel against the top of the wooden stick. Poke the pushpin through the center of the pinwheel into the stick. Blow on your pinwheel to make it spin. You may have to adjust the pin so that the wheel can spin freely.

Dangle Bead Bookmark

Make a dangle bead bookmark for summer reading using ribbon and beads.

Materials Needed

Ribbon, about 12 inches long
and 2 to 3 inches wide

Scissors

Glue stick

Needle

Embroidery thread

Small beads

1 medium-size bead

1. Cut 2 lengths of ribbon, each about 12 inches long. Lightly glue inside of both pieces of ribbon. Press the 2 pieces of glued ribbon together so that they are even on all sides.

2. Fold the top 2 corners in toward the center to make a point. Crease the ribbon lightly with your fingertips to help make the pointed shape. Dab glue on the undersides, then use your fingers to press the ribbon down firmly.

3. To make the beaded dangle string: Thread an 18-inch piece embroidery thread through a needle, and tie both ends together in a strong knot.

4. Stick the needle up from underneath near the top of the folded points, then pull it through. The knot will be hidden underneath the fold. Thread beads onto the point of the needle until you like the pattern and length of the beaded dangle. Add the medium-size bead last. When you have added the last bead, loop the needle through the bead and tie off the thread with a double knot.

Big Bubbles

Materials Needed

5 cups warm water

2 cups dish soap or laundry detergent

½ cup corn syrup (optional)

Combine the water, soap, and syrup in a large bowl. Pour some of the mixture in a shallow pan, dip in your wand and blow bubbles. If you have leftover solution, store it in a covered plastic or glass container.

Bubble Wands

You can also use a drinking straw or a small funnel as a bubble blower or make a wand from thin wire shaped in a circle or a triangle. Wrap the wire around a small stick or plastic straw to make a handle.

Bubble Cone

Materials Needed

1 sheet 8 ½-by-11-inch construction paper

Masking tape

Scissors

Roll the paper into a cone shape and secure it in the middle with masking tape. Trim top and bottom of the cone to create even edges. The cone should stand upright if the trim is even. Dip the wider end of the cone in a small bowl of bubble solution, and blow gently from the narrow end. Try long slow exhaling to make larger bubbles.

Bubble Art

Add several drops of food coloring to the bubble mixture, and blow bubbles onto white paper to make bubble art.

Five-Pointed Star

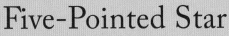

Legend has it that in June 1776 Betsy Ross, a patriot and seamstress, suggested the design of a five-pointed star to General George Washington for the nation's flag because she could make a star in one snip. Once you master how to fold and cut a five-pointed star, you can make them any size. Use them to decorate your bicycle for Independence Day, to make a star garland or a flag.

Materials Needed

1 sheet 8 ½-by-11-inch white paper

Red and blue markers

1. Take a sheet of 8 ½-by-11-inch paper and fold in half widthwise (Fig. 1). Crease the top fold firmly with your fingertips. The paper should measure 5 ½ by 8 ½ inches.

2. Fold down the top of the paper in half again, and crease along the top. Unfold so that the paper is back to 5 ½ by 8 ½ inches (Fig. 2). The middle crease that you just made will be your guide for the next step.

3. Bring the top right hand corner over to the left center crease. The point of the corner should hit the middle crease (Fig. 3). Crease well.

4. Fold the right top corner back and over to align with the outer right edge (Fig. 4). The outer edges should be even. Crease well.

5. Next, take the outer top left corner and fold it across to meet the inside left fold (Fig. 5). It should look like Fig. 6. Crease well.

6. Turn paper over and fold the small left flap to the right, over the triangle shape, to meet the edge (Fig. 7). You should have a pointed shape that looks like Fig. 8.

7. Mark a cutting line as shown in red in Fig. 8. Cut from right to left up along your marked line to make the final shape.

8. Open up the smaller cut piece and view your five-pointed star! Decorate with stars and stripes.

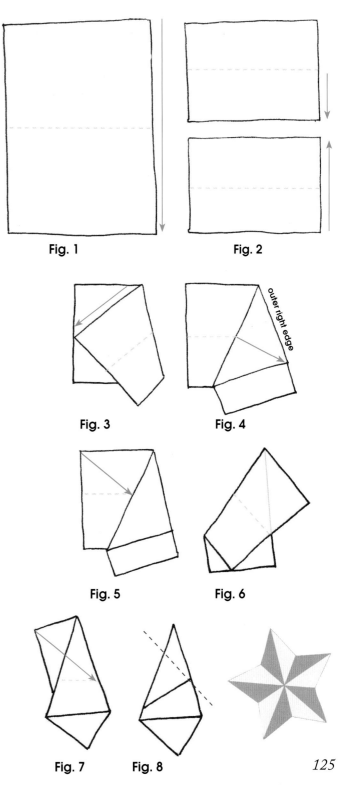

Fig. 1   Fig. 2

Fig. 3   Fig. 4

Fig. 5   Fig. 6

Fig. 7   Fig. 8

4th of July Confetti Blower

Get your friends together to make these Independence Day confetti blowers.
Bring them to a 4th of July parade or a back yard picnic.

Materials Needed

2 sheets 8 ½-by-11-inch red or blue construction paper

Scissors

Glue stick

Clear tape or stapler

Confetti

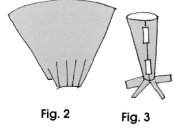

Fig. 1

1. Fold 1 sheet of a paper in half lengthwise then cut along the fold. You will have 2 strips of paper. Set aside 1 strip for later.

2. From the other strip, punch or cut a hole about ½ inch wide near the base of one of the short ends of the paper. Roll this strip into a tube. Glue the long edges together. Tape or staple the end nearest the hole flat (Fig. 1). This will be the pipe stem for the confetti blower.

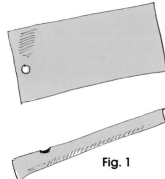

Fig. 2   **Fig. 3**

3. For the bowl of the pipe, cut a 4-inch square from the other strip of paper and fold in half. Trim left and right edges so they are shaped like a fan (Fig. 2).

4. Make 4 evenly spaced cuts on the bottom then roll the paper into a funnel shape (Fig. 3). Tape or staple the edges of funnel together. Open the small prongs at the bottom and spread over the pipe hole as shown. Glue firmly into place (Fig. 4). Fill the pipe bowl with confetti, and blow.

Fig. 4

5. To make confetti cut red, white, blue, and silver paper into small squares or paper punch into dots.

Paper Hat

Make a patriotic paper hat to celebrate the 4th of July. Use white paper, and decorate the hat with stars and stripes. You can also use folded newspaper or recycled wrapping paper.

Materials Needed

1 sheet 11-by-17-inch construction paper or newspaper

1. Fold a sheet of paper lengthwise to meet the bottom edge of the sheet. Crease the fold firmly with your thumb. It should be 8 ½ by 11 inches (Fig. 1).

2. Fold in half again from left to right, and crease (Fig. 2). Open up to the 8 ½-by-11-inch shape.

3. Fold down top left corner to align along the center fold (Fig. 3). Crease well along the outer diagonal fold. Repeat the same steps for the top right side. The two sides will fold to make a point. This will be the top of the hat.

4. To make the bottom flap, fold one side of the bottom edge upward to cover the folded triangle side of the hat (Fig. 4). Turn the hat over and fold up the other side to be even with other fold. Decorate with streamers, stickers, and stars.

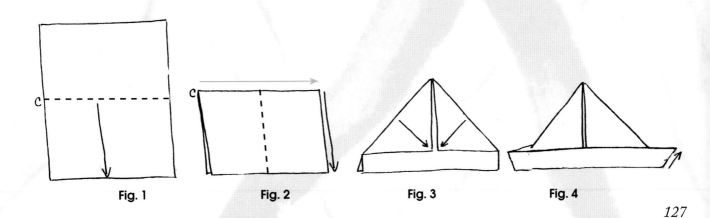

Fig. 1   Fig. 2   Fig. 3   Fig. 4

Quill Pen

In the days before ink pens were invented, people used feathers dipped in ink to write their letters or to keep family records. After you've made a quill pen, try it for writing notes in your feather journal.

Materials Needed

1 large feather

Craft knife

Washable ink

Paper

1. Using a regular pen, outline a triangle shape at the point of the feather quill.

2. With Adult Help, use a craft knife to cut along the triangle to form a sharp point at the base of the feather.

3. Dip the feather pen in watercolor or black ink. The ink should seep up into the quill. Refill frequently as you practice your penmanship.

Feather Collecting

Walking in the woods is a great way to discover hidden treasures from nature, especially feathers. There are so many varieties to collect and identify. To help you classify and label your collection, you might want to invest in a bird identification book that is specific to your region of the country. When scouting for feathers, look in areas where birds feed, bathe, and nest. Remember, do not touch or disturb the birds or their nests.

Feather Journal

Materials Needed

Letter-size envelopes for storing feathers

Three-ring binder

Guidebook for identification

Construction paper, a variety of colors

Clear tape

Watercolors or colored pencils

1. You will want to take several letter-size mailing envelopes with you on your walk. When you find a feather, place it in the envelope for protection until you get home.

2. When mounting your feathers, use one sheet of construction paper for each feather. Mount your feather with tape and label it. Store the finished pages in a binder or make a scrapbook (see page 134) to fit your design.

Extra Ideas: To make your feather collection more interesting you could collect according to color or feather markings. It is also fun to make a watercolor or drawing of your feather or write a journal entry about your walk and which birds you observed.

Directions

Having a sense of direction out of doors is useful for every beginning hiker or camper. Here's a simple way to make yourself a compass and learn north, south, east, and west.

Stand facing the sun in the morning, spread your arms straight out from your shoulders. In front of you is east; behind you is west; to your right hand is south; to the left north.

Magnetic Compass

It's easy to make a magnetic compass if you have a refrigerator magnet, a steel or iron needle, and a small bowl of water. The magnetic field of the Earth causes a magnetized needle to move into a north-south position.

1. Fill a shallow plastic or ceramic bowl with water. Rub a sewing needle (any size) in one direction over a magnet then rub the needle carefully on the side of your nose. The needle is now magnetic, and the oil from your skin will help the needle float on the surface of the water.

2. Gently place the needle on the surface of the water in the bowl. The needle will float in the water and pivot until it points to magnetic north. If you move the bowl in a different direction the needle will reposition itself to magnetic north.

Extra Ideas: Place the magnetic needle inside a small straw or through a sliver of cork to help it float on top of the water.

Paper Drinking Cup

When you go out on a picnic or hike, you should always have a drinking cup.
Here's a clever way to make one from a sheet of paper. Do not use paper that
has printing on it, as there is danger of being poisoned from the ink.

Material Needed

1 sheet clean white or brown paper

1. Cut a clean sheet of paper into an 8-inch square. Fold it in half diagonally to form a triangle (Fig. 1).

2. Lay the folded paper—now a triangular shape—on a flat surface with the folded edge toward you. The top of the triangle should point away from you.

3. Fold the right corner of the triangle upward to meet the left side (Fig. 2). The angle should be 90 degrees. Crease the right fold well.

4. Next, fold the left corner upward to overlap on the right side (Fig. 3). Crease well.

5. Fold the top corner downward (Fig. 4). Turn over and fold the other top corner downward. Gently open the center with your index finger and thumb. Fill your little cup with water or juice. Remember to dispose of the cup properly.

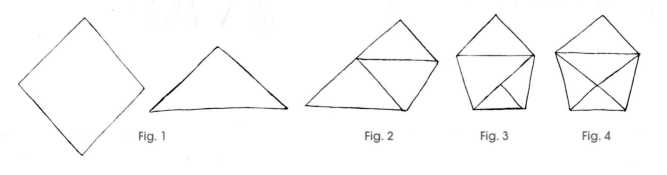

Fig. 1   Fig. 2   Fig. 3   Fig. 4

Seashell Candles

Keep the glowing days of summer going by making candles using shells collected on the beach. Large clam shells are the best for seashell candles, but smaller shells with open cavities also make great summertime candles. Always have an adult help you when working with hot wax or using matches.

Materials Needed

Clam shells

1 tablespoon vinegar

8-ounce empty soup can, cleaned

Medium-size saucepan

Bits of old candles (light pink, blue or green if possible) or paraffin wax

Wick

Oven mitt

1. Soak the shells for about 20 minutes in a bowl filled with clean water and vinegar. Drain the shells and air dry them in the sun.

2. Set out newspapers on a work surface and place the shells on top. Cut about a 2-inch length of wick for each shell.

3. With Adult Help, place soup can in a saucepan of water. Add the candles or paraffin wax to the can and turn heat on medium-low. Heat until wax melts.

4. With Adult Help, use the oven mitt to carefully pick up the heated can of wax. Hold the wick in the middle of the shell with one hand and then carefully pour the hot wax into the shell. **Be sure not to touch the hot wax!** After pouring the wax, set the can aside in a safe place to cool.

5. Hold the wick in place for 1 to 2 minutes, or until the wax has set. Trim the top of the wick as needed. Let the candles cool for 1 hour or until all the wax beneath the surface has hardened.

Extra Ideas: Set the shell candles in a shallow bowl of water. **With Adult Help**, light the candles.

Treasure Jar

If you are spending any time near the ocean this summer, be sure to collect a treasure jar of shells, pebbles, and ocean glass left on the beach by the waves. Store tiny shells, bits of sand, pebbles, and ocean glass in little glass jars so you can always remember summer by the ocean.

Summer Travel Scrapbook

Putting together scrapbooks is a classic tradition during summer vacation. Make one to hold all of your memories from camp and family trips. Collect souvenirs like maps, brochures, napkins, postcards, sugar packets, and travel tickets from memorable places. When you get home from vacation, make a homemade scrapbook. Use homemade paper to make a unique cover.

Materials Needed

2 sheets 8 ½-by-11-inch handmade paper
or decorative paper

Metal-edged ruler and craft knife

10 sheets 8 ½-by-11-inch construction
paper or natural colored printing paper

Scissors

Small hammer

Thin nail or awl

Rubber band

Shoelace

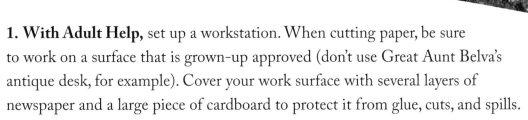

1. With Adult Help, set up a workstation. When cutting paper, be sure to work on a surface that is grown-up approved (don't use Great Aunt Belva's antique desk, for example). Cover your work surface with several layers of newspaper and a large piece of cardboard to protect it from glue, cuts, and spills.

2. To make a cover, select a heavy paper and trim 2 pieces to 8 ½ by 11 inches, the same as your text paper.

3. Place text sheets between covers. Wrap a rubber band around the top to secure the covers and papers before punching holes in the binding.

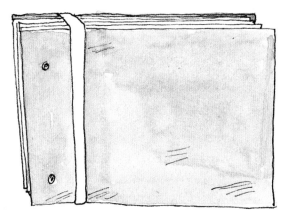

4. Mark symmetrical holes about 1 inch in from the edge. Use the hammer and nail to punch a hole through each mark. The nail should pierce front cover, pages and back cover. Be sure the nail is large enough to allow the shoelace or ribbon to pass through the holes.

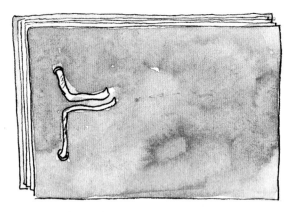

5. Push a shoelace through one of the holes from the underside to the top. (You want to be sure that it goes through the paper holes as well as the cover.) Bring the shoelace over to the other hole and push the lace through to the back. Tie the lace into simple tight knot. Make sure the lace is tight enough to keep the book together but loose enough for you to open the pages and add to your scrapbook pages. Attach a charm, seashell, some beads, or feathers to the string for added decoration, then tie a bow. You can also wrap a different sheet of decorative paper, about 5 by 8 ½ inches, over the spine before punching the holes.

More Fun with Scrapbooks

To store letters, photos, or a feather or leaf collection, glue the back of a letter-size or square envelope to the page or inside cover. Store the items inside the envelope. Decorate the outside of envelope with labels, cut-out letters, stickers, or rubber stamps.

Use corrugated cardboard for the cover and paint or collage pictures on the front and back.

Decorate with buttons, flowers, pictures, seeds, stickers, bits of fabric, and pictures from an old book—whatever you like to make it unique.

Watercolor a white shoelace for the binding to make it colorful.
You can also use ribbon or string instead of a shoelace for the binding.

Arrange a series of fun photos that you took of your friends and family and write a brief story about the photos.

Be creative! Anything goes when you're making a scrapbook.

Drawstring Field Bag

Make a field bag from old cotton pants to carry a notebook, pencil, compass, or any item you might need for an afternoon hike or a high adventure. Personalize with patches, embroidery, buttons or beads. Burlap or muslin sacks also can be used to make great bags.

Materials Needed

Old pair of cotton pants

Scissors

Straight pins

Large-eyed needle and strong thread

Cord, about 40 inches long

1. Cut off a pant leg just below the knee. If possible, use a pair of pants that has pockets below the knee. After you cut off the pant leg, you will have two seams from the original pant leg on either side, and a hemmed-open bottom.

2. Turn the pants inside out. Use the up-and-down stitch (see page 106) to create a seam, or a closure along the top of the pant leg. This will be the bottom of your bag (Fig. 1). The original hem from your pants will be the bottom of your bag.

3. Still working inside out, cut a 2-inch slot at the top left side of the original hem (Fig. 2). Fold down one side about ½-inch until you create a tunnel or casing. Your string will slide through this tunnel. Pin in place above the fold to keep seam in place and stitch.

4. Cut a cord about 40 inches long. Take one end of the cord and attach it to a safety pin. Push the safety pin through one side of the casing and pull the ribbon through until you have ribbon on each side. Tie the ends in a knot and pull to close your field bag (Fig. 3).

Fig.1

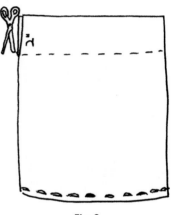

Fig.2

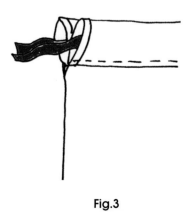

Fig.3

Fig.4

Animal Track Casting

Casting animal tracks is a perfect hobby for someone who enjoys collecting and making things from nature. Look for animal tracks near muddy banks where wild animals might drink or feed. Spring, summer, and fall are the best seasons for casting tracks. You will want to have a field bag for your supplies (see page 138), or one that you can sling over your shoulder or across your chest.

Materials Needed

Field or shoulder bag for carrying materials

Strips of cardboard

Paperclips

Package of plaster of Paris

Mixing container

Water

Mixing spoon or stick

1. When you find a track, clear away twigs and small stones so that the track is clearly visible. Use 2-inch cardboard strips to form a fence around the track. Paperclip the ends of the cardboard together to form your mold.

2. In a container, mix water into plaster and stir until the paste has the consistency of melted ice cream. Pour about 1 inch of plaster into the cardboard mold.

3. Let the plaster harden for about 30 minutes. Gently remove the cardboard and place on newspaper. Wrap the cast loosely in newspaper to protect it.

4. When you get home, let it dry completely. Label the back of each cast with the date, location, and type of track.

Campfire Stories

The campfire is a golden opportunity for the
telling of stories—good stories told well.
Indian legends, war stories, ghost stories,
detective stories, and stories of heroism.
The history of fire and a talk about the stars
will fascinate even the youngest listener.
Don't drag out the telling of a story.
Make the story live!

Toasting Marshmallows

When the embers are glowing, it's time for
toasting marshmallows. Get a long stick sharpened to
a point, fasten a marshmallow on the end, hold it over
the embers, not in the flame, until the marshmallow
expands and turns a golden brown.

Back-Yard Camping

Back-yard camping is a great way to have a big adventure.
If you don't have a tent and a sleeping bag , you can build a lean-to
made from a blanket or tarp and lay blankets on the ground.
Here's an old-fashioned idea for an outdoor bed:

1. Find a spot in the yard that has two trees close together. Tie a rope between the two at about shoulder height.

2. Using an old blanket or tarp as a cover, cut a hole in each corner of the tarp. Cut 4 lengths of string about 12 inches long. Push one piece of string through each hole and tie a secure knot. Attach a small stick or garden stake to the end of each rope. Each string will have a stake attached.

3. Drape the covering over the string between the two trees. Pull the bottom corners tight to the ground and pound in the stakes. Pull the top strings tight to the ground in front. You may have to add more rope to reach the ground. Pound in the stakes.

4. On the floor of your lean-to, lay a thick layer of the branches of balsam fir or hemlock, with the convex side up, and the butts of the stems toward the foot of the bed.

5. Be sure to make the head of your bed away from the opening of the lean-to and the foot toward the opening. Spread your sleeping blanket over top the evergreens. You will be surprised how soft and fragrant a bed you will have.

INDEX